draw me a house

THIBAUD HEREM

THESE ARE DIFFERENT TYPES OF HOUSES
FROM AROUND THE WORLD

FAMILY HOUSE, NEW ENGLAND, USA

COUNTRYSIDE BARN, SWEDEN

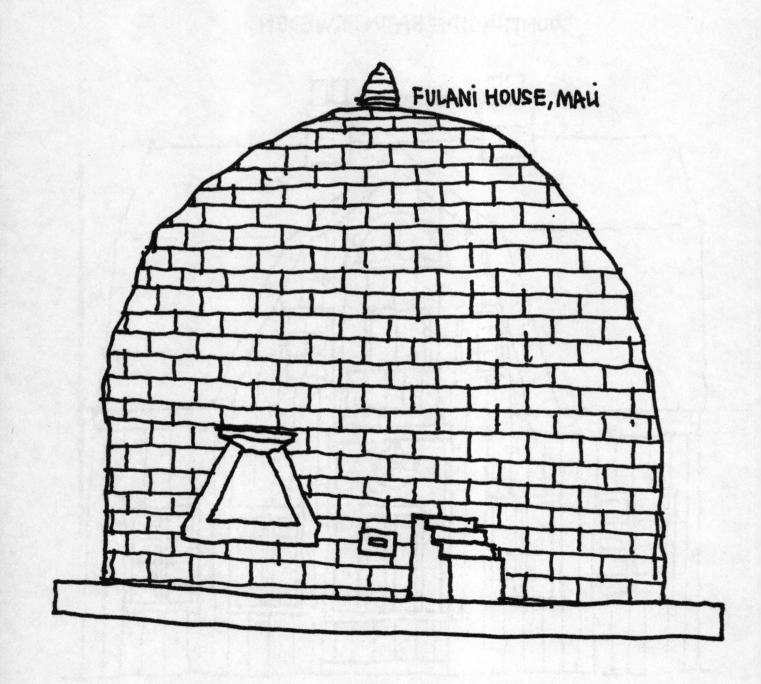

FULANI HOUSE, MALI

DRAW THE HOUSE YOU LIVE IN

DOORS

THE WAY YOU ENTER A BUILDING CAN MEAN A LOT.
DOORS CAN WELCOME YOU IN OR SHUT YOU OUT.
DRAW THE HOUSES THAT THESE DOORS BELONG TO

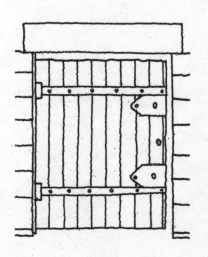

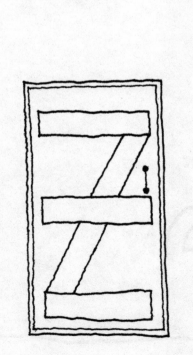

PROPORTIONS ARE IMPORTANT TO CONSIDER.

THESE TWO HOUSES ARE EXACTLY THE SAME EXCEPT
THAT ONE HAS A BIG DOOR AND ONE HAS A LITTLE DOOR.

DRAW THE WINDOWS TO GO WITH EACH HOUSE

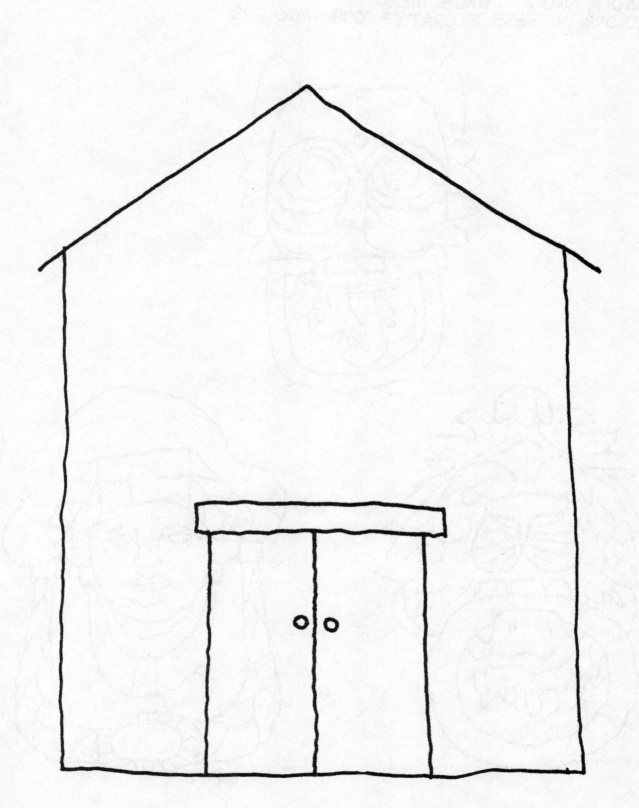

DOOR KNOCKERS

KNOCK KNOCK... WHO'S THERE?
COLOUR IN THESE DECORATIVE DOOR KNOCKERS

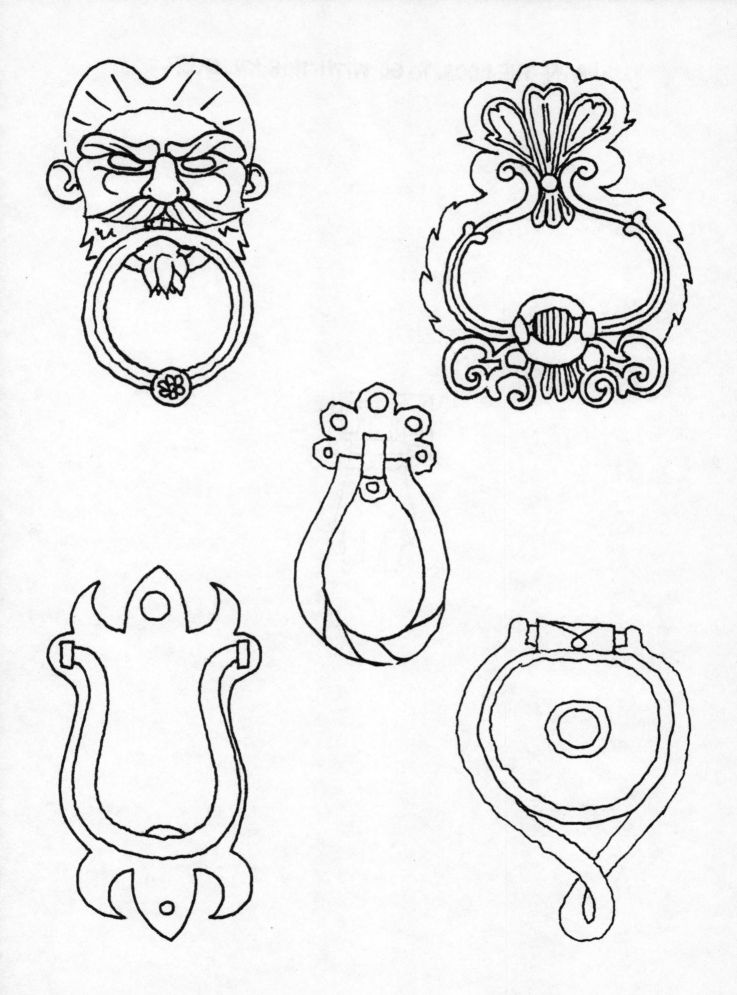

DRAW A KNOCKER TO GO ON THIS DOOR

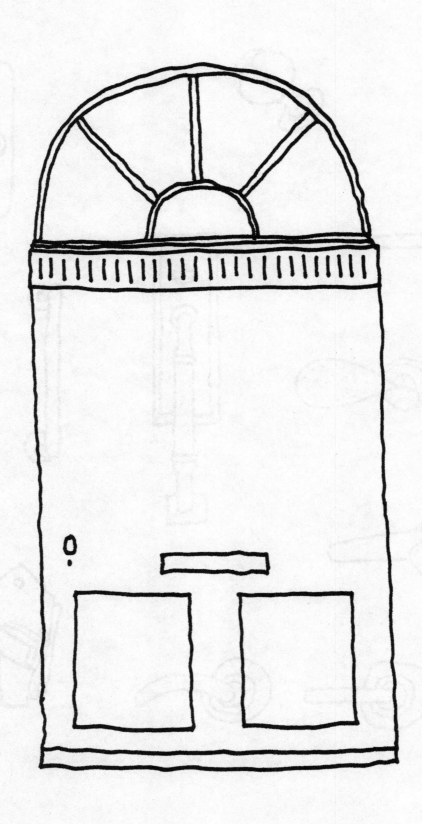

GET A HANDLE ON IT! CHECK OUT THESE DECORATIVE
DOOR HANDLES. WRITE UNDERNEATH EACH ONE WHAT
YOU THINK IT'S FOR. IS IT FOR AN INTERNAL DOOR?
AN OUTSIDE DOOR? A CUPBOARD? A DRAWER?
A MAGICAL WARDROBE TO THE WORLD OF THE UNKNOWN?

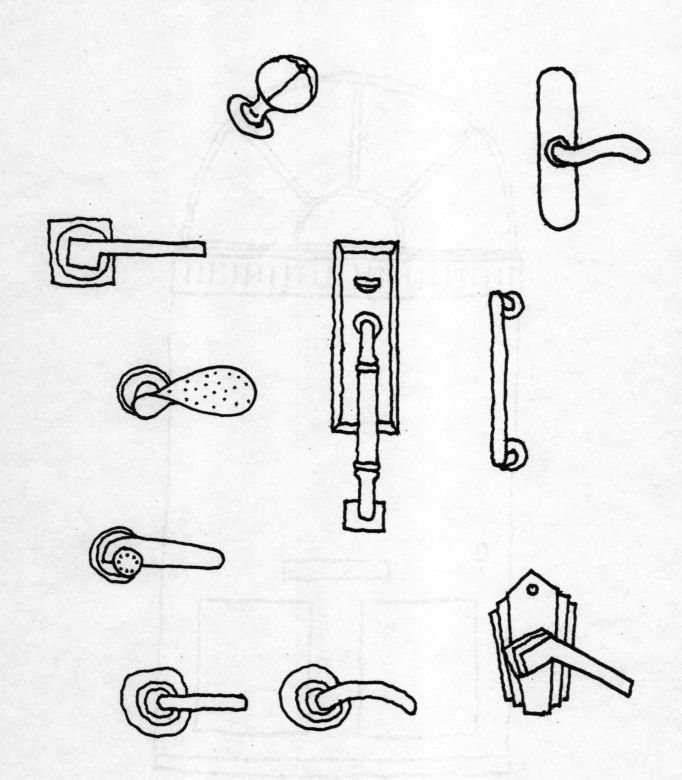

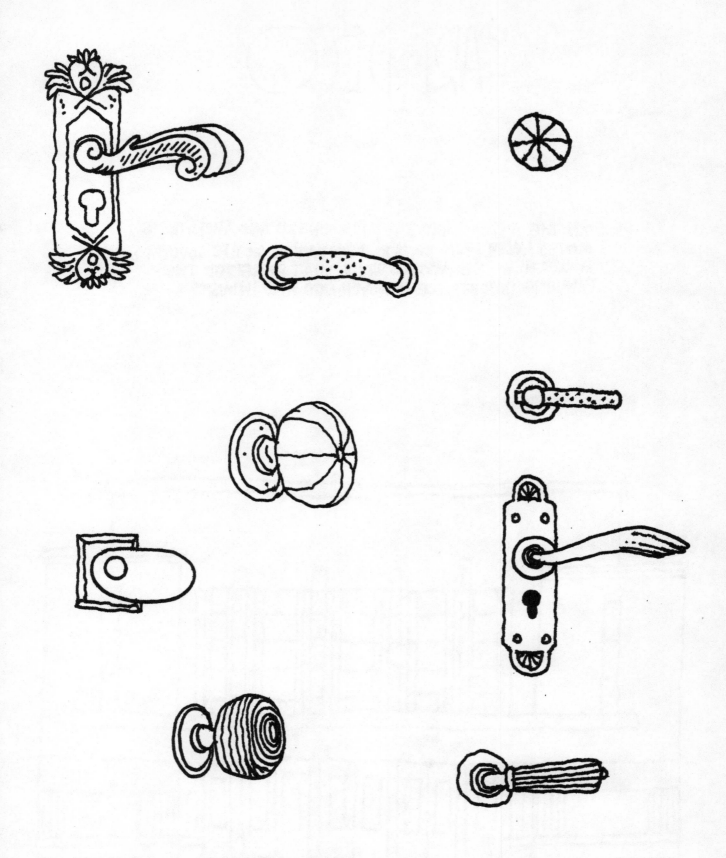

ART DECO

IN THE 1920s AND 30s, DESIGNERS AND ARCHITECTS MOVED AWAY FROM ORNATE DECORATIVE MOTIFS TOWARDS A CLEANER, GEOMETRIC STYLE THAT REFLECTED THE GROWING IMPORTANCE OF MACHINES AND INDUSTRY

ART DECO CINEMA

IMAGINE HOW GLAMOROUS AND STRANGE THESE HOUSEHOLD
OBJECTS MUST HAVE LOOKED WHEN THEY FIRST CAME OUT...

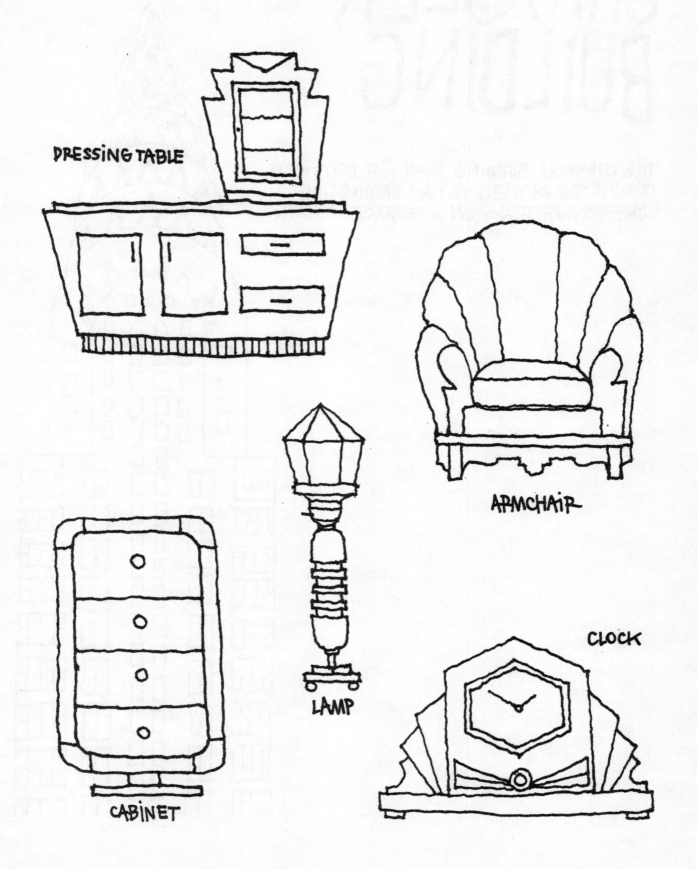

DRESSING TABLE

ARMCHAIR

LAMP

CABINET

CLOCK

CHRYSLER BUILDING

THE CHRYSLER BUILDING IS AN ART DECO ICON.
COMPLETED IN 1930 IT HAS DISTINCTIVE
SUNBURST PATTERNS ON A TERRACED CROWN

HOW WOULD IT LOOK WITH A DIFFERENT TOP ?

THIS IS A CROSS SECTION OF PART OF A VERY TALL SKYSCRAPER.
DRAW WHAT'S HAPPENING ON EACH FLOOR

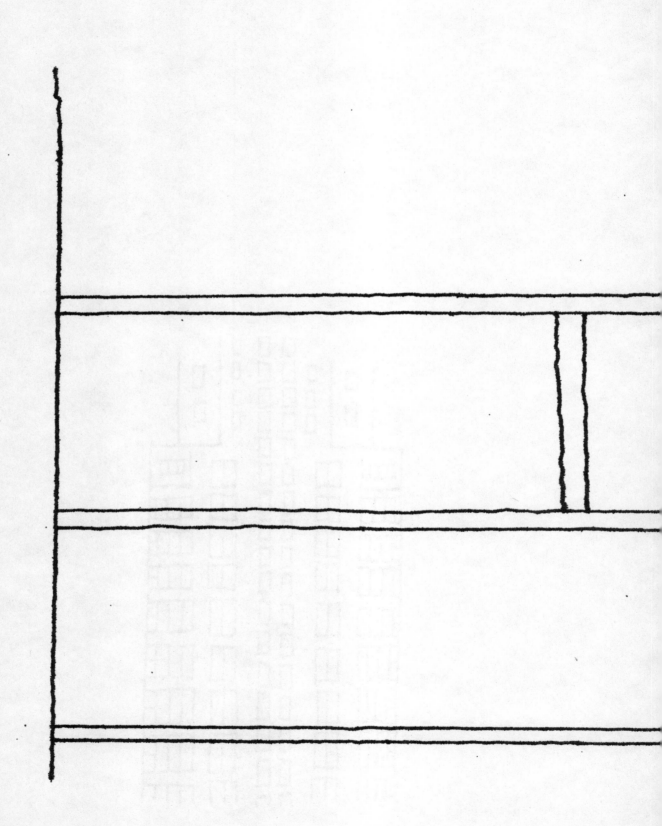

COLOUR IN THESE HOUSEBOATS

IMAGINE SAILING YOUR HOUSE DOWN A CANAL ON A
WARM SUMMER'S DAY

DRAW A NARROWBOAT TO CALL YOUR OWN

DRAW THE INSIDE OF THE NARROW BOAT. WHAT CLEVER
SPACE - SAVING IDEAS HAVE YOU GOT TO FIT IN ALL
THE MODERN CONVENIENCES ?

WALLPAPER CAN BRING A ROOM TO LIFE.

DECORATE THE KITCHEN AND LIVING ROOM WALLS
WITH WALLPAPER — DON'T HOLD BACK — MAKE IT WILD!

IN JAPAN, TRADITIONAL HOUSES HAVE A LIFESPAN OF 20
OR 30 YEARS, AND THEN THEY ARE TORN DOWN.
INSIDE, THE HOUSES HAVE A FLEXIBLE LAYOUT. ANY ROOM
CAN BE USED FOR ANY PURPOSE — A BEDROOM, A DINING ROOM,
A STUDY... FOR THIS REASON ALL THE FURNITURE IS PORTABLE
AND CAN BE STORED AWAY IN A LARGE CLOSET CALLED AN OSHIIRE.

DRAW A ROOM INSIDE THIS TRADITIONAL JAPANESE HOUSE.
THINK WHAT TYPE OF FOLDABLE FURNITURE YOU MIGHT USE

FRANK LLOYD WRIGHT
TOOK AN ORGANIC APPROACH TO ARCHITECTURE
FITTING HIS BUILDINGS INTO THE SURROUNDING NATURE

FALLINGWATER, COMPLETED IN 1935, IS A MAGNIFICENT
PRIVATE HOUSE BUILT OVER A WATERFALL IN PENNSYLVANIA

DRAW A HOUSE THAT FITS INTO THIS LANDSCAPE

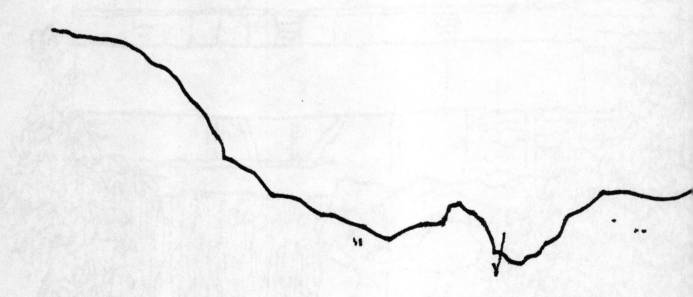

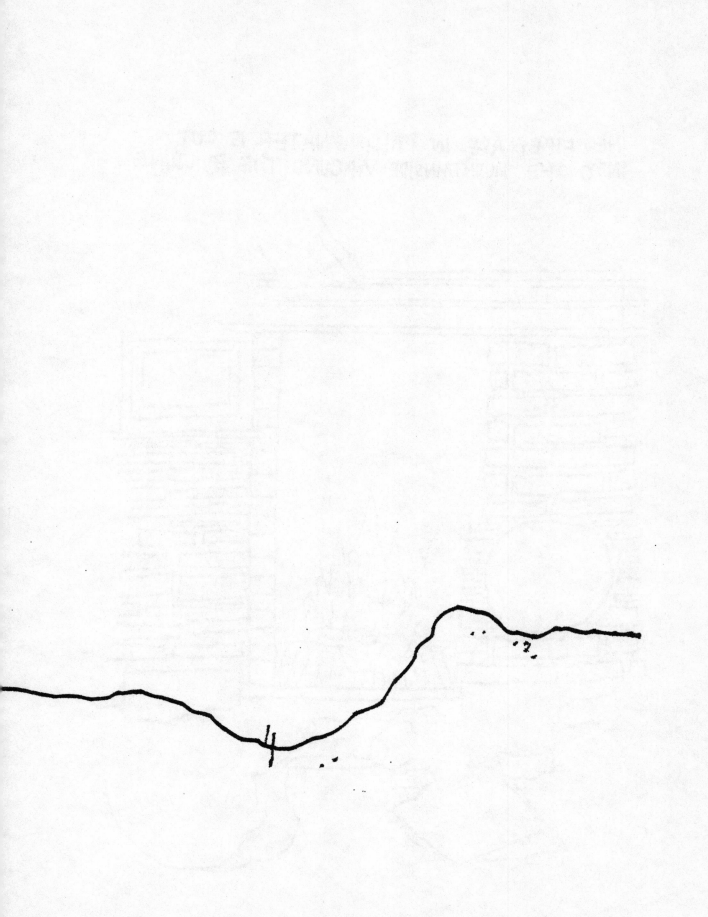

THE FIREPLACE IN FALLINGWATER IS CUT
INTO THE MOUNTAINSIDE AROUND THE BUILDING

DRAW YOUR OWN FANTASY FIREPLACE

CHAIRS ARE AT THE HEART OF MODERN FURNITURE
DESIGN - REFLECTING NEW TECHNOLOGIES, CULTURAL
DEVELOPMENTS AND THE VISIONS OF DESIGNERS WHO
USED THE HUMAN FORM FOR INSPIRATION

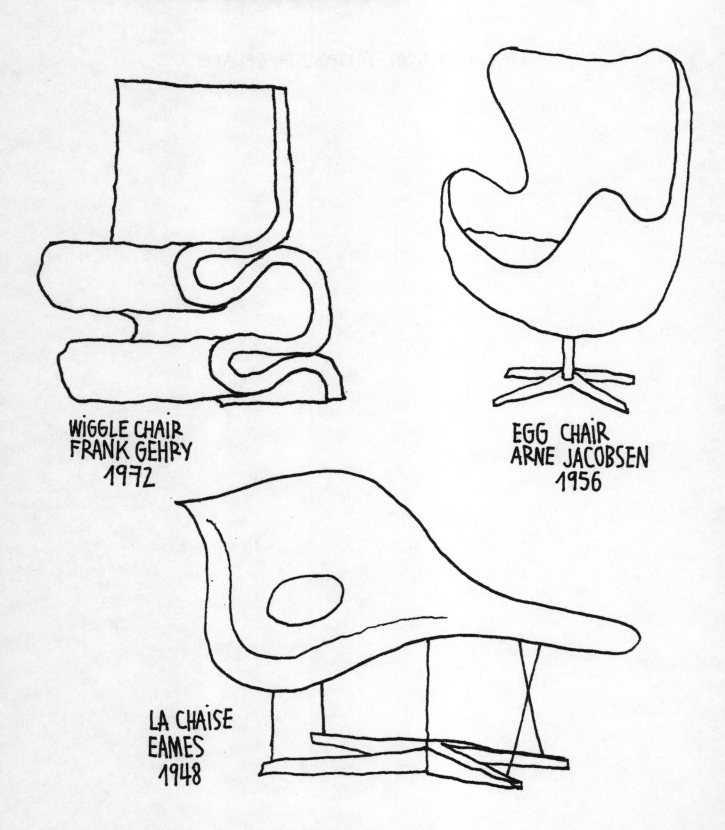

WIGGLE CHAIR
FRANK GEHRY
1972

EGG CHAIR
ARNE JACOBSEN
1956

LA CHAISE
EAMES
1948

STACKING CHAIR
ROBIN DAY
1963

BALL CHAIR
EERO AARNIO
1963

LC3 ARMCHAIR
LE CORBUSIER
1928

DRAW THREE DIFFERENT CHAIRS.
A DINING CHAIR, AN ARMCHAIR AND A SOFA FOR TWO

PLAYGROUNDS USE THE LAWS OF PHYSICS:
GRAVITY, BALANCE, CENTRIFUGAL FORCES TO CREATE
A FUN ENVIRONMENT

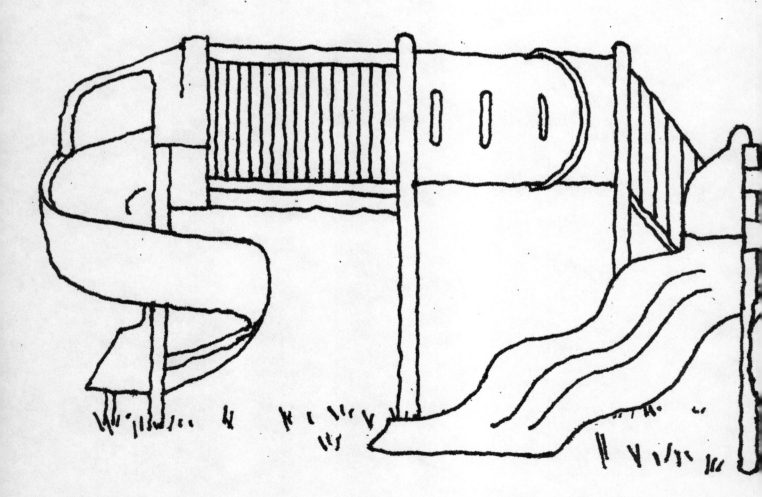

DRAW A FANTASTIC SEE-SAW FOR YOU
AND YOUR BEST FRIEND TO PLAY ON

DRAW A HOUSE TO SUIT EACH ONE OF THESE FRIENDLY MONSTERS

DRAW THE MONSTER THAT LIVES IN THIS BIZARRE ABODE

BEFORE WRISTWATCHES BECAME COMMONPLACE, CLOCKTOWERS WERE AN IMPORTANT CENTRAL FEATURE OF TOWNS AND VILLAGES

COLOUR THESE CLOCKTOWERS IN
AND DRAW ON SOME
DECORATIVE CLOCKFACES

TREEHOUSES

DRAW YOUR DREAM TREEHOUSE HERE —
DON'T FORGET TO FURNISH IT COMFORTABLY!

THIS HOUSE IS BUILT IN A TREE TO PROTECT THE OCCUPANTS FROM SCAVENGING ANIMALS AND FLOODING

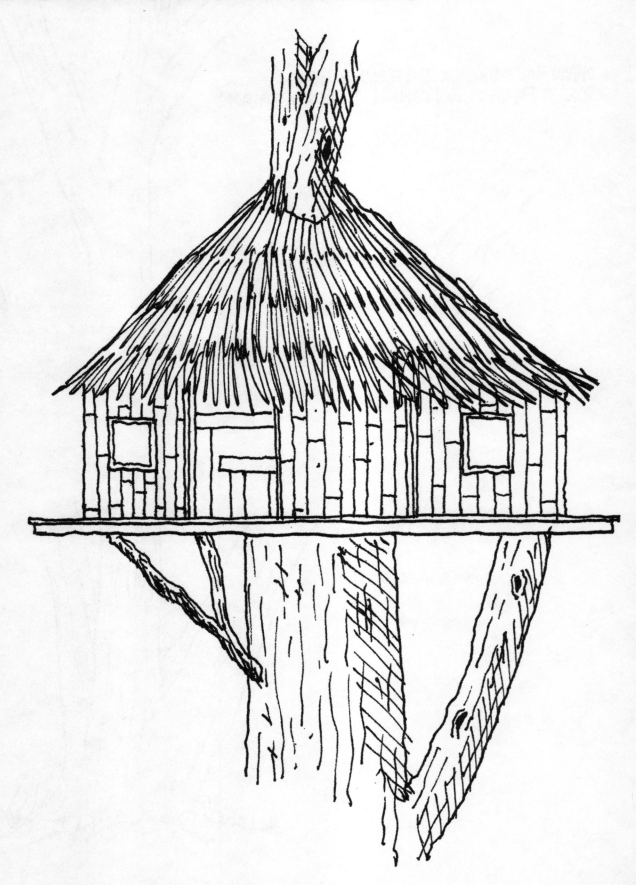

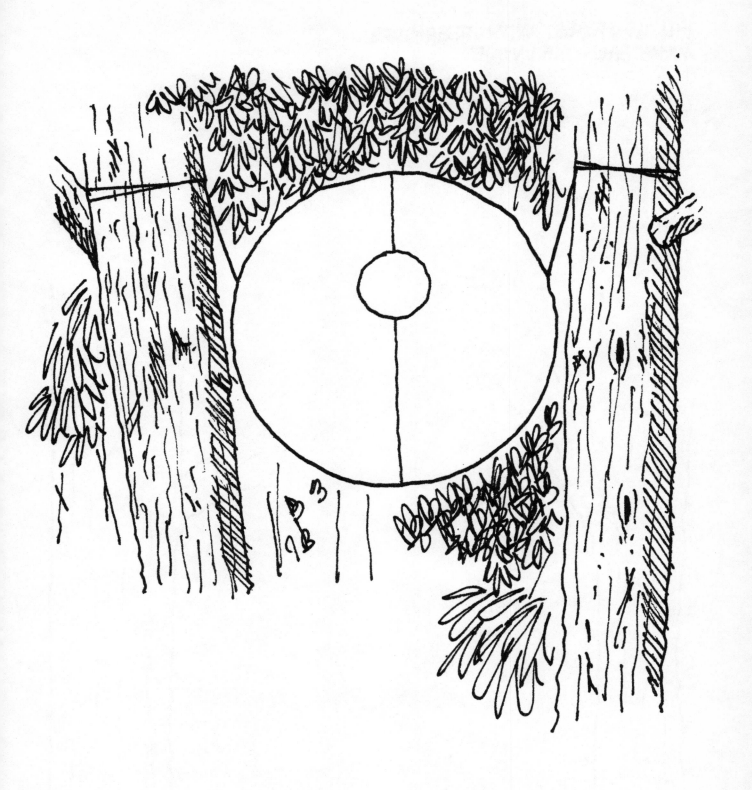

THIS TREEHOUSE IS A PLACE OF CONTEMPLATION FOR
A VERY CONTEMPORARY DESIGNER

FILL THIS FOREST WITH TREEHOUSES.
MAKE EACH ONE UNIQUE

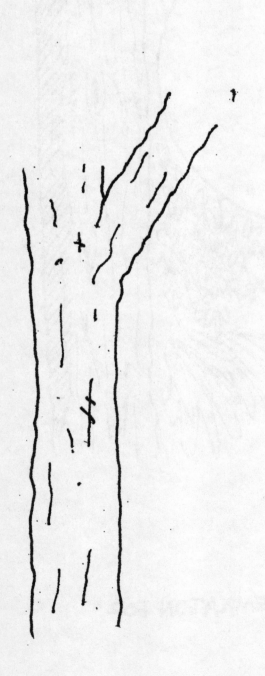
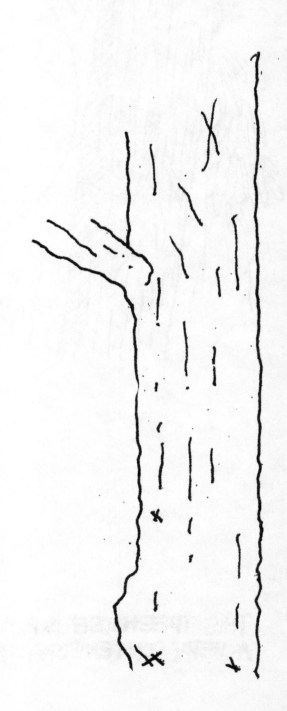

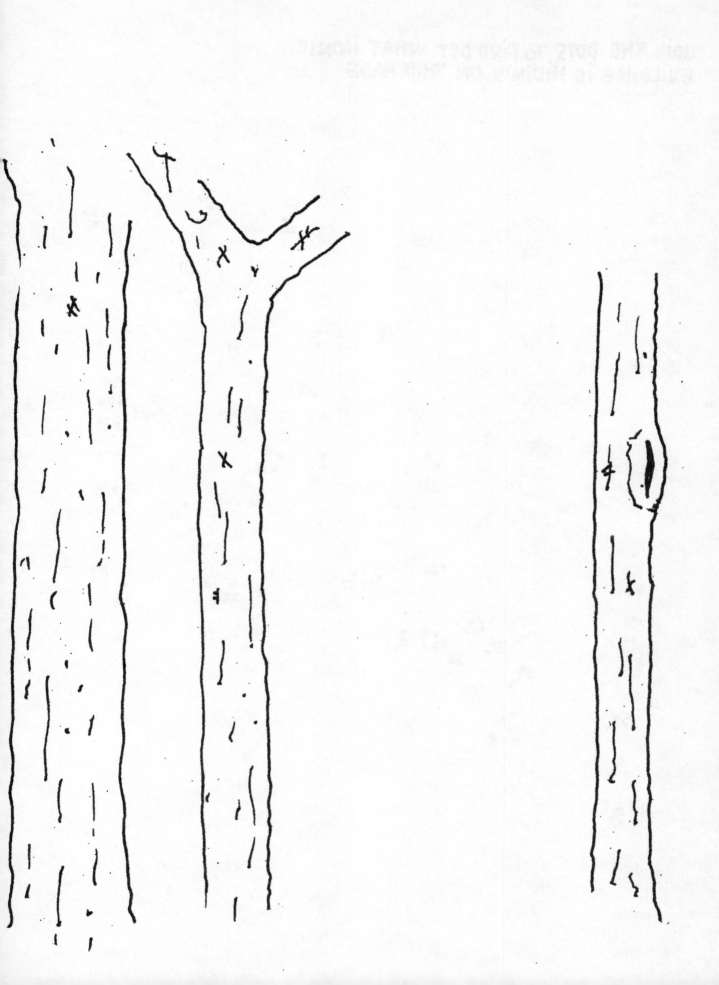

JOIN THE DOTS TO FIND OUT WHAT ICONIC
BUILDING IS HIDING ON THIS PAGE

S. . . . . O. . . . H. . . .
DESIGNED BY JØRN UTZON
1957 – 1973

36

43   44   45

42

37
47

41

38

.46   .49

40 48

51

50

52

53   .54

55

SOMETIMES ARCHITECTS NEED TO FIT THEIR DESIGNS
TO AWKWARD PLOTS AND BRIEFS

DRAW A HOUSE BETWEEN THESE TWO BIG BUILDINGS

AND SOMETIMES THEY HAVE COMPLETE FREEDOM.
DRAW YOUR FANTASY HOUSE ON THIS HUGE PLOT OF LAND

LIGHTING

CAN CHANGE THE FEEL OF A ROOM

DRAW A LAMP FOR THIS DESK

DRAW A PENDANT LAMP HANGING OVER
THIS KITCHEN TABLE

STREETLAMPS COME IN ALL SHAPES AND SIZES

TEMPORARY STRUCTURES

NOMADIC PEOPLES USED TENTS, TIPIS AND YURTS
AS THEY FOLLOWED HERDS ACROSS THE PLAINS

YURT

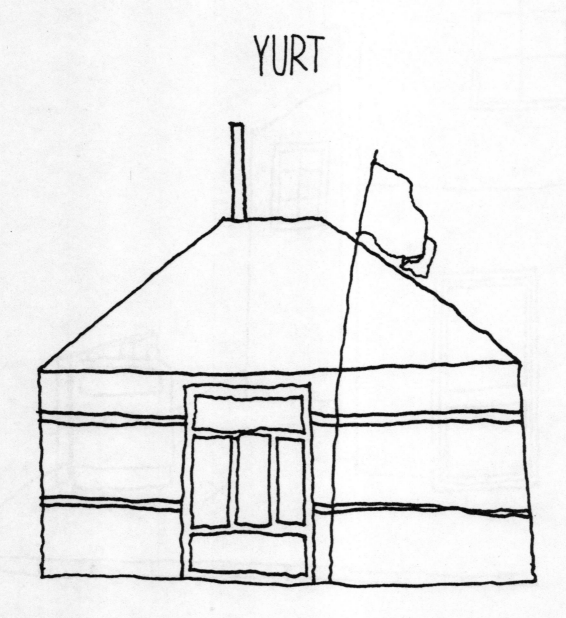

TIPI

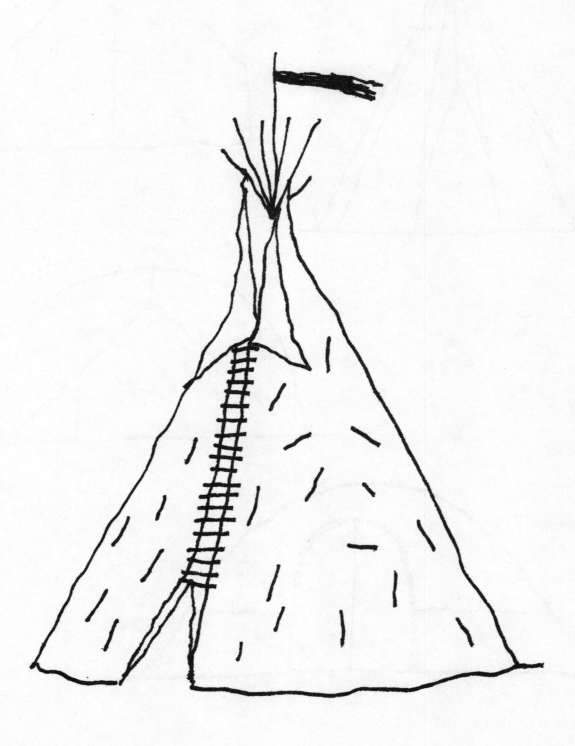

TENTS TODAY COME IN A VARIETY OF SHAPES AND MATERIALS.
DECORATE THESE SO THEY STAND OUT IN THE CROWD

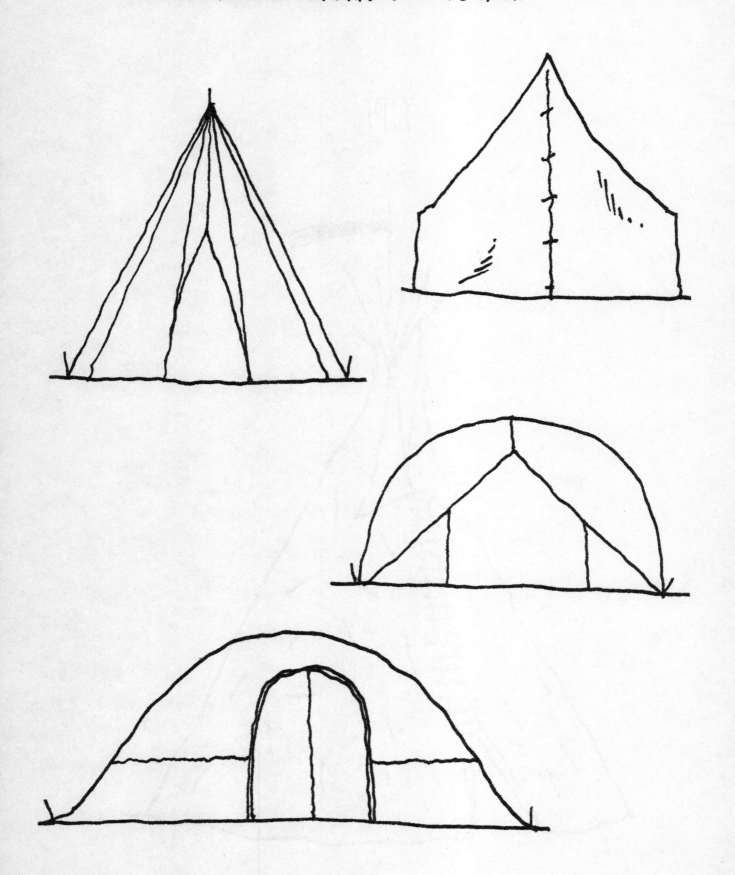

DRAW YOUR DREAM TENT FROM THE INSIDE.
MAKE IT NICE AND COSY

MOBILE HOMES
IMAGINE BEING ABLE TO TAKE YOUR HOUSE
ANYWHERE YOU WANT TO GO

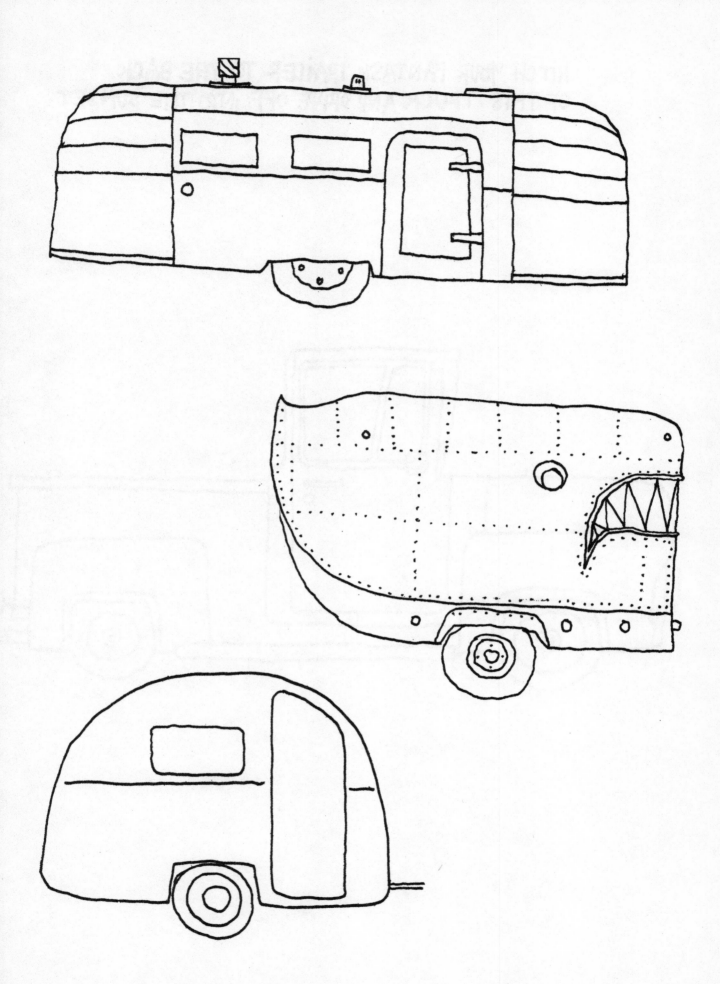

HITCH YOUR FANTASY TRAILER TO THE BACK
OF THIS TRUCK AND DRIVE OFF INTO THE SUNSET

THE DEVIL'S IN THE DETAIL!

YOU MIGHT NOT NOTICE ALL THE LITTLE DESIGN ELEMENTS THAT YOU HAVE IN YOUR HOUSE. LOOK AT THESE TAPS! WHICH ONES DO YOU LIKE?

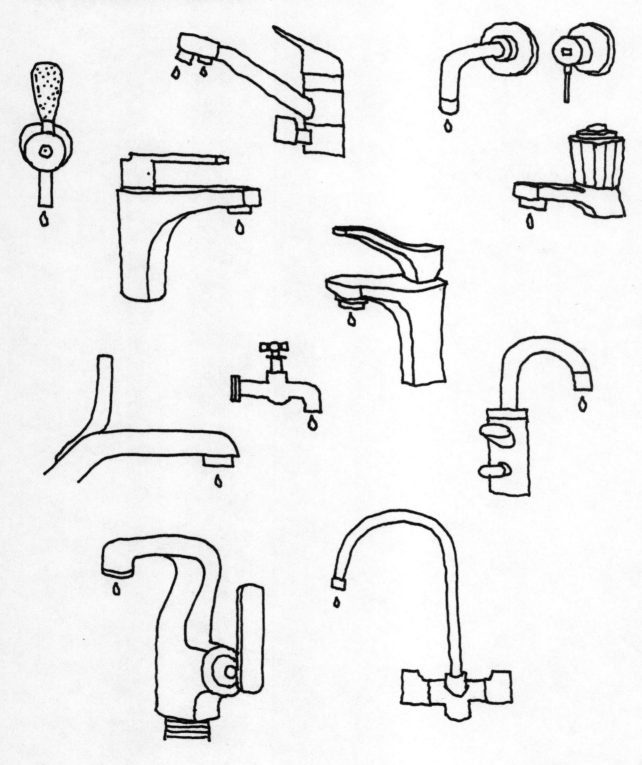

DRAW THE TAPS ON THIS BATHTUB

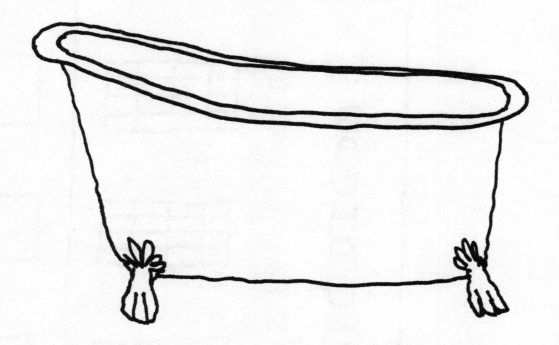

THE MODERNISTS OF THE EARLY 20TH CENTURY
SAID THAT FORM SHOULD FOLLOW FUNCTION. IN OTHER
WORDS THE LOOK OF A BUILDING SHOULD BE
INFORMED BY ITS PURPOSE

THE BAUHAUS WAS AN ART AND DESIGN SCHOOL
AT THE FOREFRONT OF THESE MODERNIST IDEALS

THE BAUHAUS BUILDING IN DESSAU WAS DESIGNED BY WALTER GROPIUS, AND WAS COMPLETED IN 1925 JUST 13 MONTHS AFTER WORK STARTED

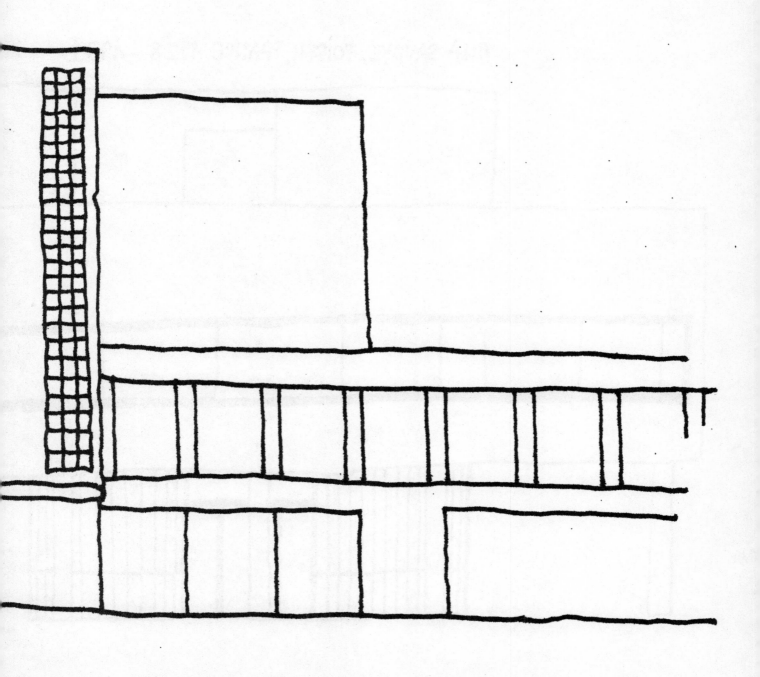

LE CORBUSIER WAS A SWISS-FRENCH ARCHITECT AT THE HEART OF THE MODERN MOVEMEMENT. HE FAMOUSLY STATED THAT THE HOUSE SHOULD BE "A MACHINE FOR LIVING IN"

VILLA SAVOYE, POISSY, FRANCE. 1928 - 1931

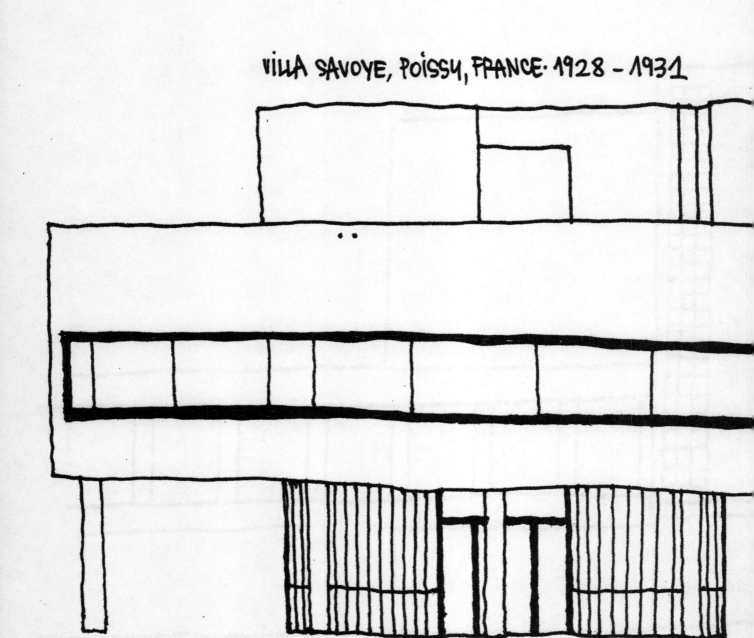

DRAW A MACHINE FOR LIVING IN

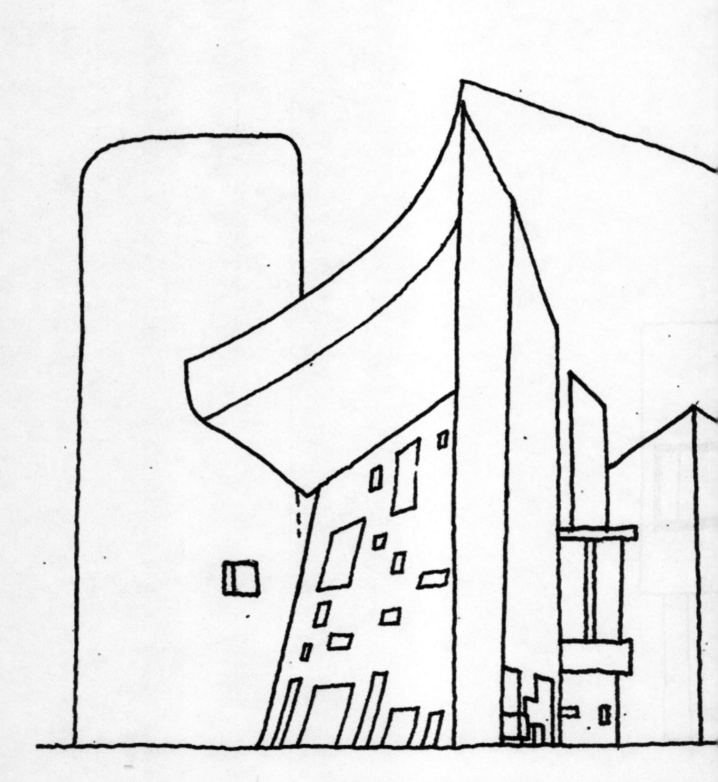

LATER IN LIFE, LE CORBUSIER MOVED TOWARDS A MORE
EXPRESSIVE STYLE OF ARCHITECTURE. NOTRE DAME DU HAUT IS
A CHAPEL THAT HE DESIGNED IN 1955. IT USES A PRIMITIVE,
SCULPTURAL STYLE TO REFLECT OUR RELATIONSHIP TO FAITH
AND COMMUNITY

GARGOYLES ARE DECORATIVE FEATURES IN THE SHAPE OF FANTASTICAL ANIMALS, BUT THEY ALSO SERVE A FUNCTION — TO KEEP RAINWATER FROM COLLECTING ON THE ROOF.

COLOUR THESE ONES IN

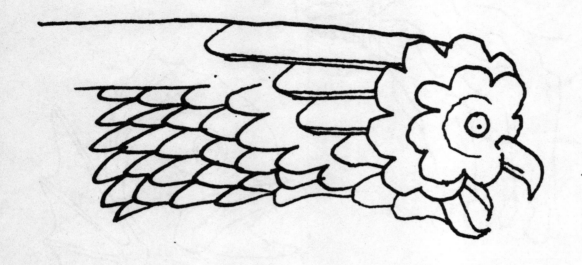

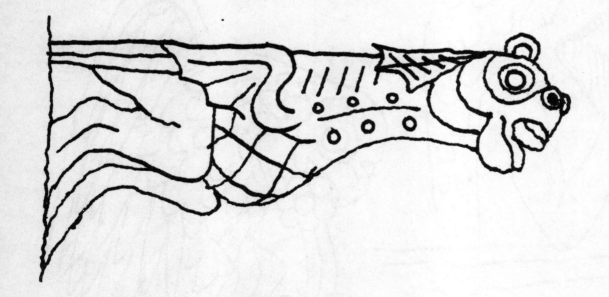

DRAW YOUR OWN GARGOYLES HERE.
ARE THEY FRIENDLY OR SCARY?

WINDOWS

WINDOWS ARE THE EYES OF BUILDINGS.
THROUGH THEM WE SEE THE WORLD OUTSIDE,
AND SOMETIMES THE WORLD OUTSIDE CAN SEE US

OEIL DE BOEUF WINDOW.

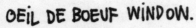

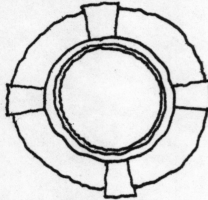

CASEMENT WINDOW.

HALF GLAZED WINDOW.

WOODEN FRAME WINDOW

I SPY WITH MY LITTLE EYE...
WHAT'S HAPPENING BEHIND THESE WINDOWS?

DRAW THE WINDOW OF THE ROOM
YOU ARE IN RIGHT NOW

DRAW THE WINDOWS BELONGING TO THIS HOUSE

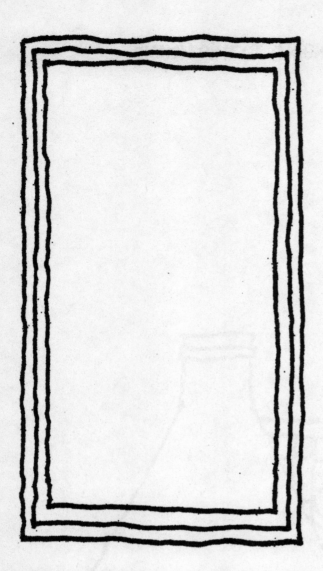

DRAW THE VIEW FROM THIS WINDOW
ON THE 20TH FLOOR OF A TALL BUILDING

DRAW THE VIEW FROM THIS BASEMENT WINDOW

SHUTTERS

EXTERIOR WINDOW SHUTTERS CAN BE FOUND
THROUGHOUT EUROPE. MAKE THESE ONES COLOURFUL!

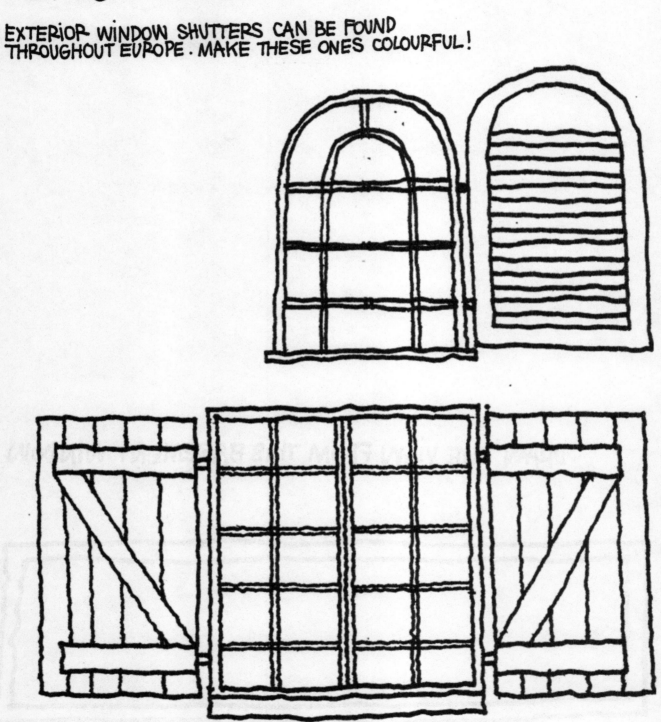

DRAW YOUR OWN WINDOW WITH SHUTTERS,
THINK SHAPE, PATTERN AND COLOUR!

BRUTALIST ARCHITECTURE MAKES NO BONES ABOUT
THE NUTS AND BOLTS OF ITS CONSTRUCTION. USUALLY
MADE OF ROUGH CONCRETE, IT HAS AN UNCOMPROMISING
BLOCK-LIKE GEOMETRY

THE BRUTALIST ARCHITECTS THOUGHT THAT THROUGH
ARCHITECTURE THEY COULD CREATE COMMUNITIES
BASED ON SOCIAL EQUALITY

TRELLICK TOWER, 1966-1972. ERNO GOLDFINGER

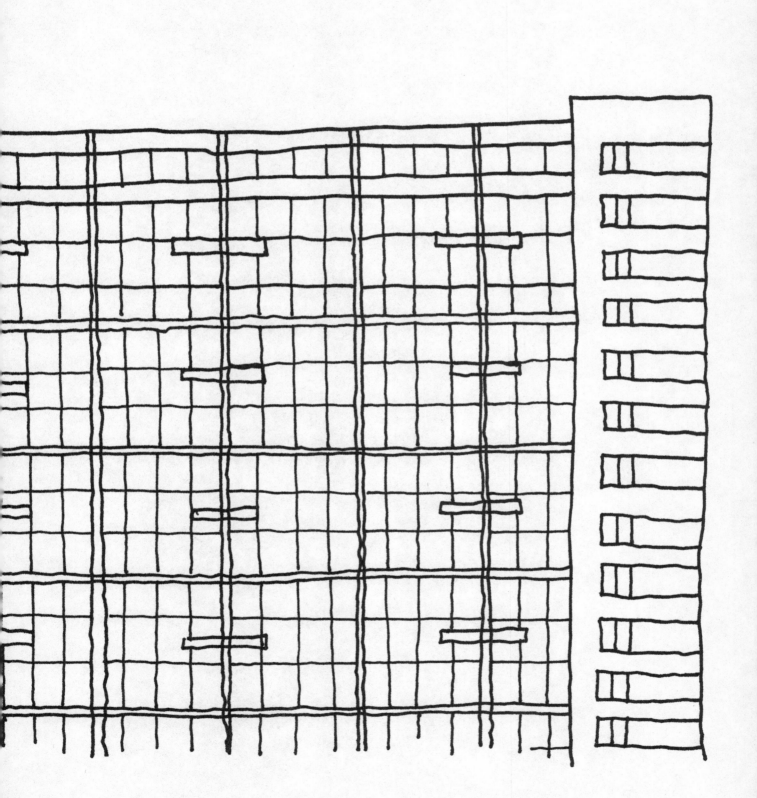

DRAW A BLOCK OF FLATS WITH SHOPPING,
ENTERTAINMENT AND COMMUNAL FACILITIES ALL ON SITE

DRAW THE REST OF THIS STREET AND COLOUR IT IN.
DON'T FORGET TO DRAW THE PEOPLE WHO LIVE ON IT

DECORATIVE ELEMENTS CAN MAKE A HOUSE A HOME.
COLOUR IN THESE VASES

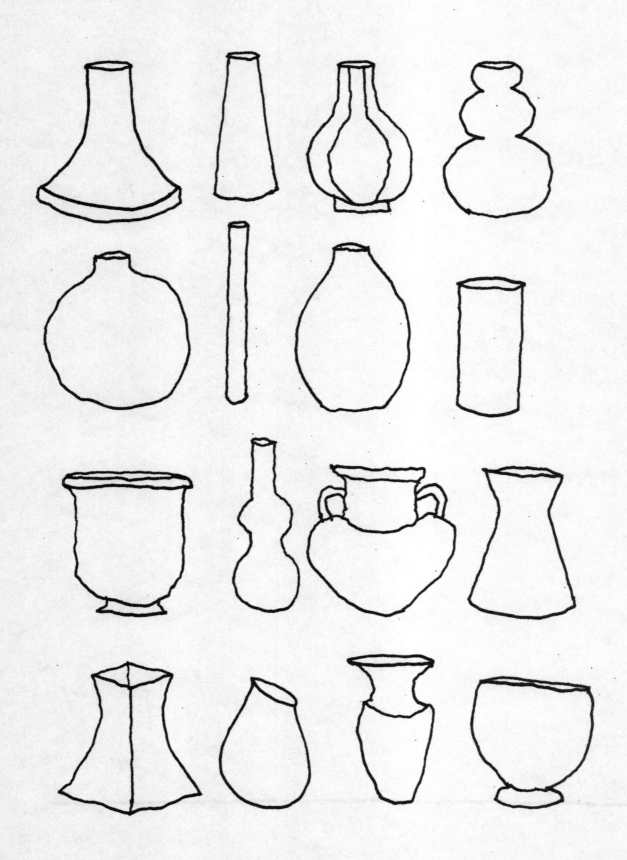

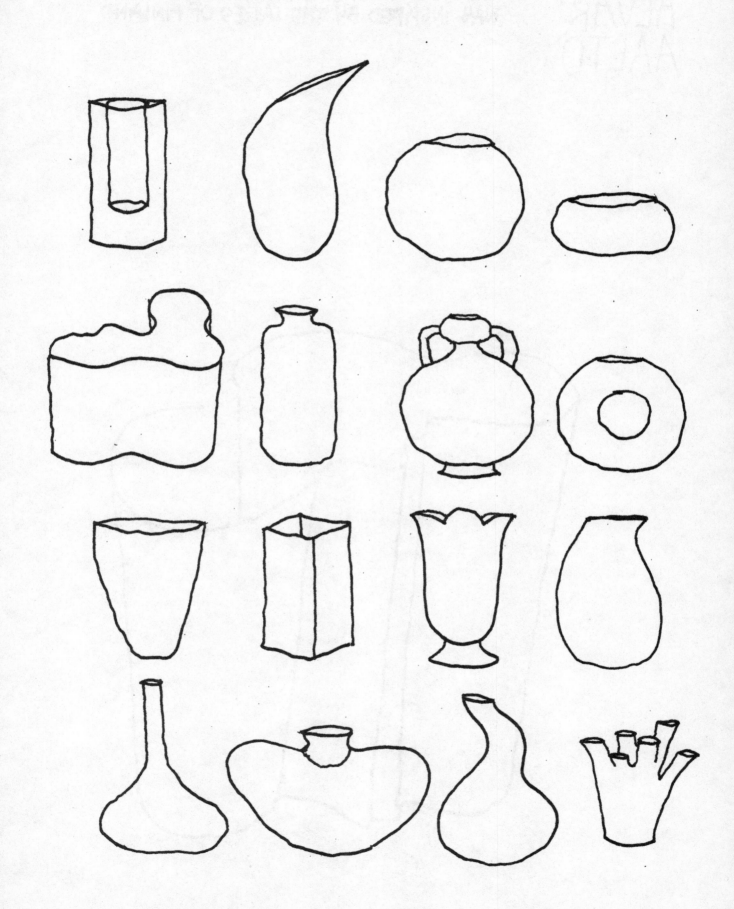

ALVAR AALTO

THIS VASE DESIGNED BY ALVAR AALTO
WAS INSPIRED BY THE LAKES OF FINLAND

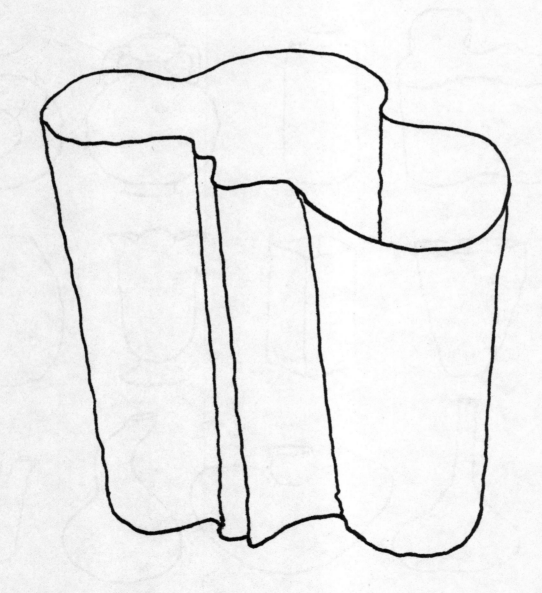

DRAW A BEAUTIFUL VASE INSPIRED
BY A NATURAL ELEMENT

DECORATE THIS LIVING ROOM. DRAW AS MANY VASES AS YOU
CAN·ON THE SHELVES. DON'T FORGET TO FILL THEM WITH
AMAZING FLOWERS

AN IGLOO IS AN INUIT HOUSE THAT USES BLOCKS OF ICY SNOW
TO CREATE AN INSULATED SHELTER. WHEN TEMPERATURES OUTSIDE
PLUNGE TO -40°C THE TEMPERATURE INSIDE CAN BE AS WARM AS
12°C WITH JUST BODY HEAT AND A SMALL LAMP AS HEAT SOURCES

BECAUSE HEAT RISES, BEDS ARE BUILT ON RAISED PLATFORMS

MUD IS A COMMON BUILDING MATERIAL IN DEVELOPING COUNTRIES. IT'S MALLEABLE, DURABLE AND FREE, AND CAN PROVIDE GOOD INSULATION FROM THE HEAT

DRAW A HOUSE THAT CAN WITHSTAND EXTREME HEAT.
WHAT INNOVATIVE COOLING TECHNOLOGIES CAN YOU THINK OF?

DRAW A HOUSE THAT CAN WITHSTAND EXTREME COLD

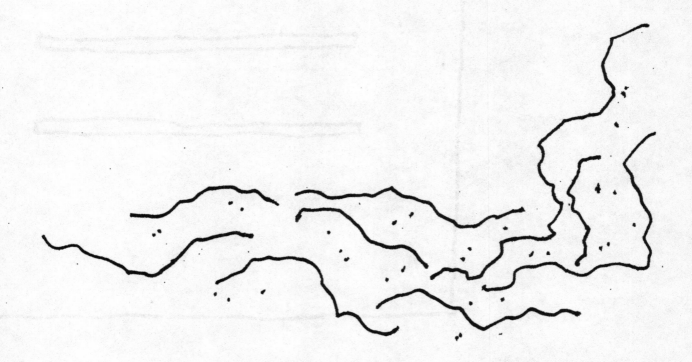

THIS IS A NUCLEAR BUNKER. STOCK IT WITH
A YEAR'S WORTH OF PROVISIONS. WHAT LUXURY
ITEMS WOULD YOU BRING WITH YOU IF YOU HAD
TO LIVE HERE FOR A YEAR?

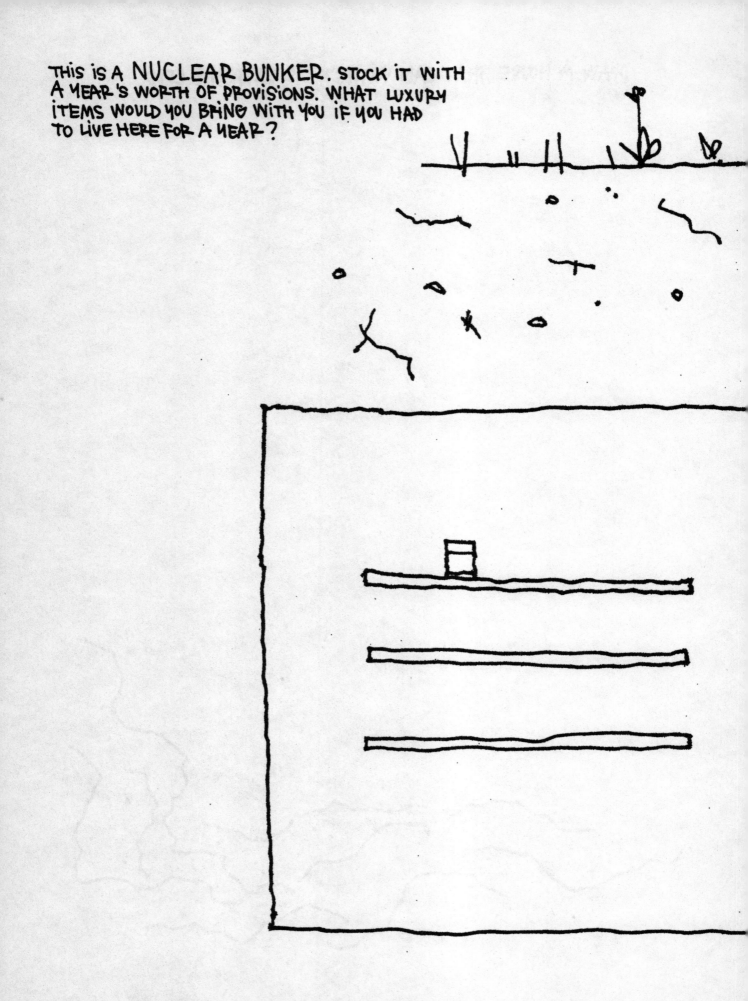

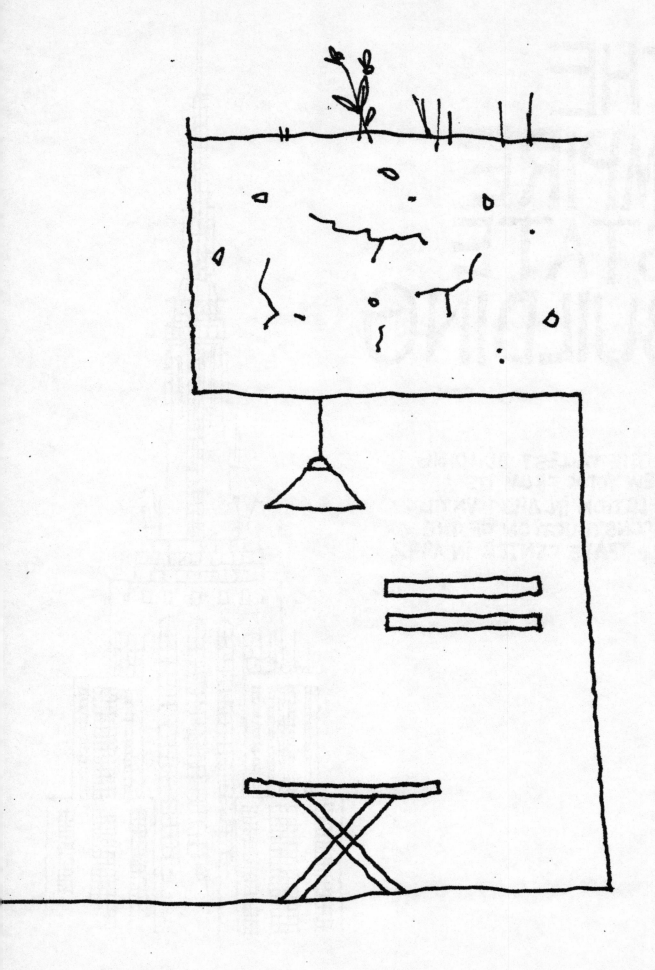

THE EMPIRE STATE BUILDING

WAS THE TALLEST BUILDING
IN NEW YORK FROM ITS
COMPLETION IN 1931 UNTIL
THE CONSTRUCTION OF THE
WORLD TRADE CENTER IN 1972

DRAW THE VIEW OF MANHATTAN FROM THE ROOF OF
OF THE EMPIRE STATE BUILDING

SKYLINES SHOW US HOW DIFFERENT BUILDINGS WORK TOGETHER TO FORM THE ARCHITECTURAL IDENTITY OF A CITY

CAN YOU GUESS THE CITY FROM THE SKYLINE...?

P....

B......

N . . . . . .

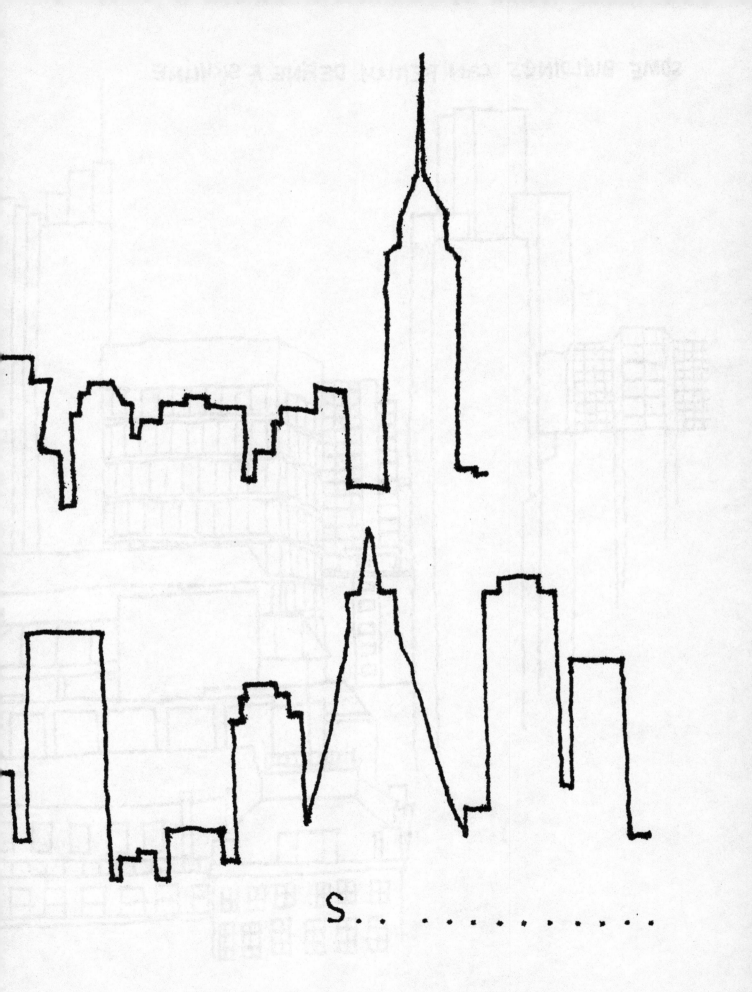

SOME BUILDINGS CAN DEFINE A SKYLINE

S.................

SOME BUILDINGS CAN REALLY DEFINE A SKYLINE

WHICH BUILDING IS MISSING IN THE LONDON CITYSCAPE?

TURN THE PAGE TO FIND OUT...

THE GHERKIN

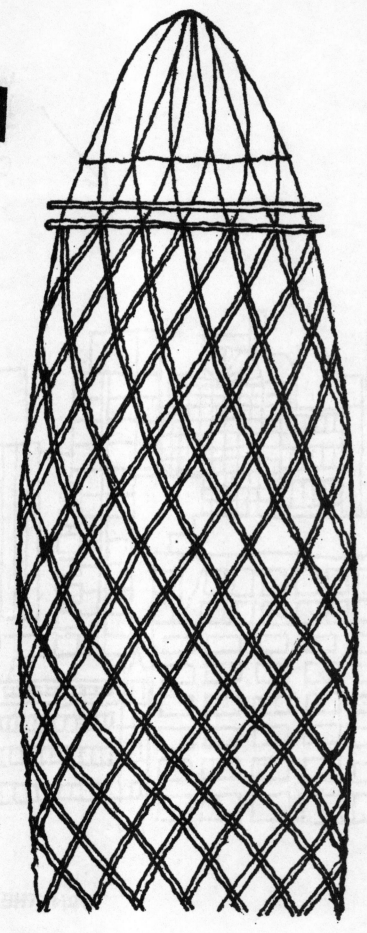

THE GHERKIN (OFFICIALLY 30 ST MARY AXE)
WAS DESIGNED BY NORMAN FOSTER AND PARTNERS.
IT USES SOME VERY CLEVER ECO-TECHNOLOGY:
* NATURAL DAYLIGHT IS MAXIMISED USING LIGHT
LEVEL SENSORS THAT PREVENT UNNECESSARY LIGHTING.
* ITS AERO-DYNAMIC SHAPE ALLOWS NATURAL VENTILATION.
* IT USES A "DOUBLE SKIN" FAÇADE WHICH CREATES SHAFTS
THAT PULL WARM AIR OUT OF THE BUILDING IN WARM WEATHER
AND WARM THE BUILDING USING PASSIVE SOLAR HEATING IN WINTER,
REDUCING THE NEED FOR HEATING AND AIR CONDITIONING.

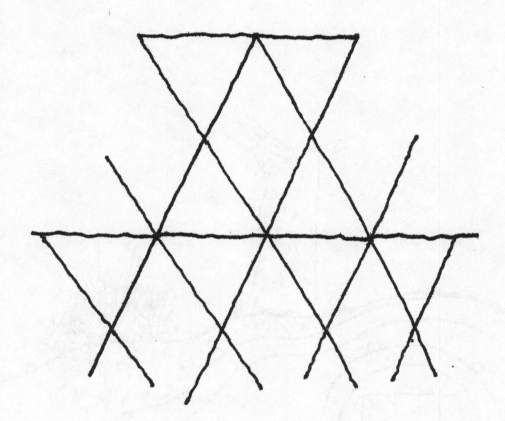

DID YOU KNOW THE ONLY CURVED
PANE OF GLASS IN THE GHERKIN IS
THE ONE AT THE VERY TOP.
ALL THE OTHERS ARE FLAT TRIANGLES

GREEN ROOFS CAN ABSORB RAINWATER AND PROVIDE INSULATION, AS WELL AS CREATING A HABITAT FOR WILDLIFE AND PROMOTING BIODIVERSITY

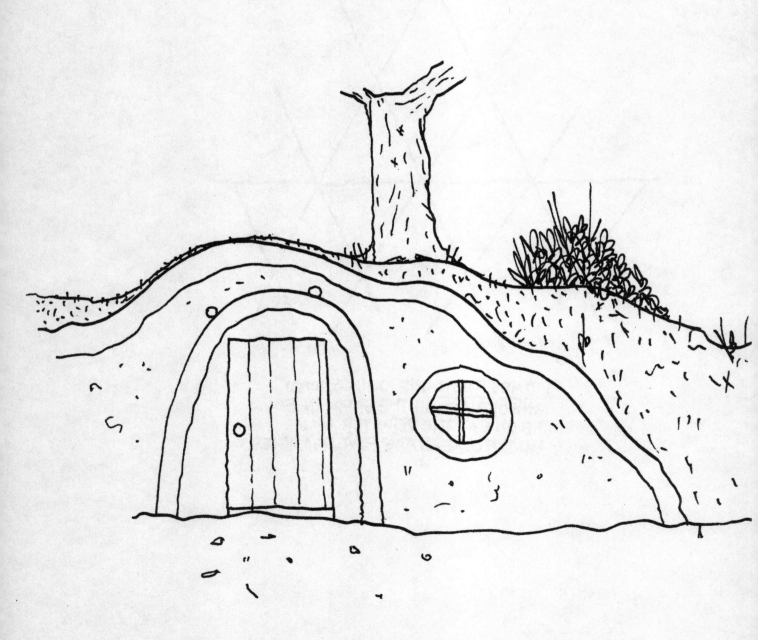

DRAW A GREEN ROOF ON THIS HOUSE

DRAW A HOUSE TOTALLY COVERED IN PLANTS AND FLOWERS
DRAW SOME OF THE INSECTS AND ANIMALS THAT MIGHT LIVE ON IT

A GREENHOUSE CAPTURES HEAT AND WATER SO THAT THE PLANTS INSIDE IT CAN FLOURISH. DRAW THE PLANTS INSIDE THIS ONE

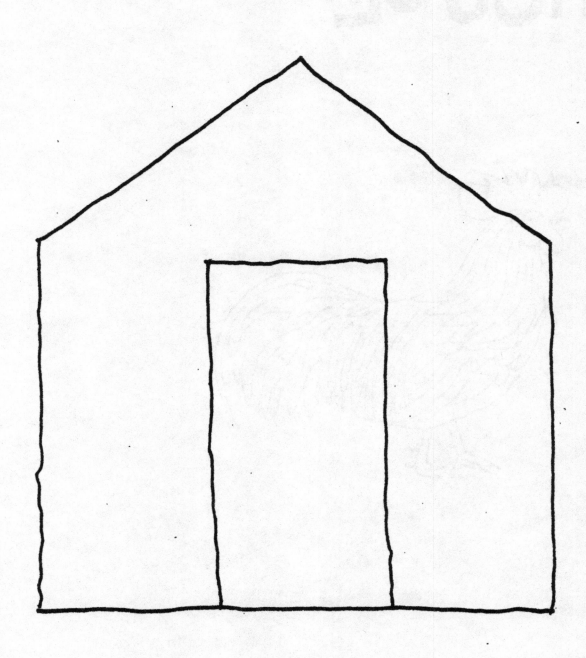

ANIMAL HOUSE

DRAW A HOUSE
FOR EACH OF THESE ANIMALS

DRAW A MAGNIFICENT DOG PALACE FOR THIS PAMPERED PUP

THESE HOUSES ALONG THE CANAL IN COPENHAGEN ARE EACH
A DIFFERENT COLOUR. COLOUR THEM IN AND THEN DRAW
THE CANAL AND THE BOATS ALONGSIDE

TILES ARE FUNCTIONAL AND DECORATIVE ALL AT THE SAME TIME!
HERE ARE A FEW NICE ONES.

THIS TILED WALL NEEDS TO BE BRIGHT AND COLOURFUL.
COLOUR THE TILES IN AND MAKE SURE THAT THERE
ARE PLENTY OF DECORATIVE ONES

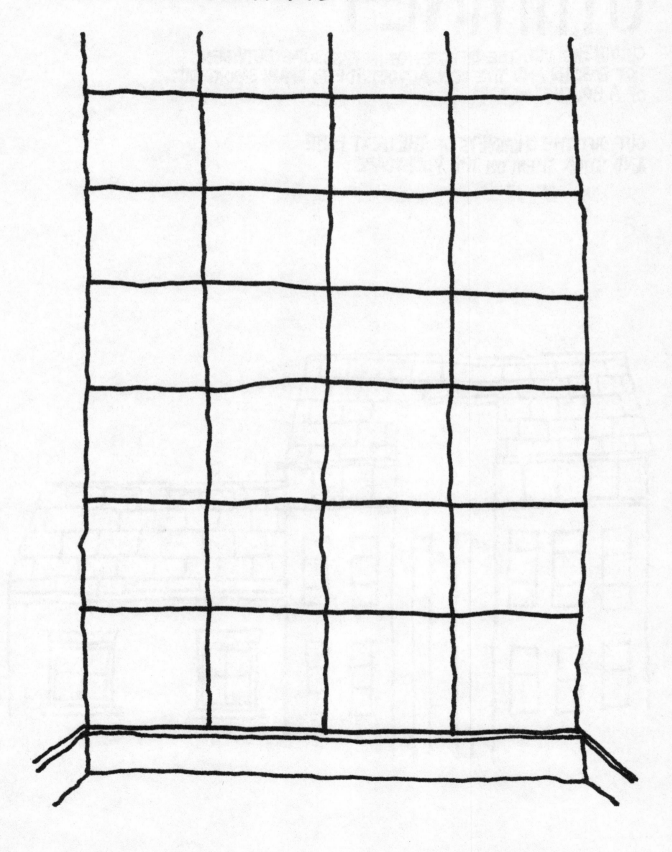

CHIMNEY

CHIMNEYS USE THE DIFFERENCE IN PRESSURE BETWEEN HOT GASSES AND THE COOL AIR OUTSIDE TO DRAW SMOKE OUT OF A HOUSE.

CUT OUT THE CHIMNEYS ON THE NEXT PAGE AND STICK THEM ON THE ROOFSCAPE

STICK MORE CHIMNEYS ON THIS ROOFSCAPE

EVEN THOUGH WE DON'T COMMUNICATE MUCH BY POST
THESE DAYS, WE STILL NEED LETTERBOXES. COLOUR
THESE ONES IN BRIGHTLY

DRAW A FUN LETTERBOX THAT WILL MAKE
YOUR POSTMAN SMILE

DRAW THE MOAT AROUND THIS MAGICAL CASTLE
DON'T FORGET THE FIRE- BREATHING DRAGON STANDING GUARD!

DRAW THE PRINCESS AND HER ROYAL FAMILY
WHO LIVE INSIDE

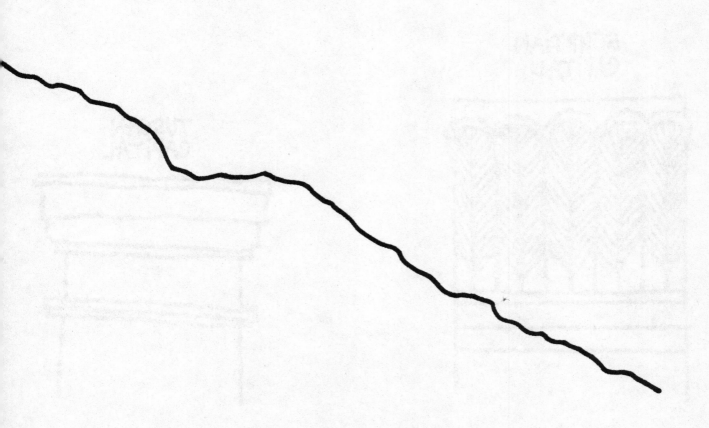

CAPITALS

CAPITALS CAN BE FOUND AT THE TOP
OF COLUMNS IN MANY TYPES OF
ANCIENT ARCHITECTURE.
THESE ARE A FEW:

EGYPTIAN
CAPITAL

TUSCAN
CAPITAL

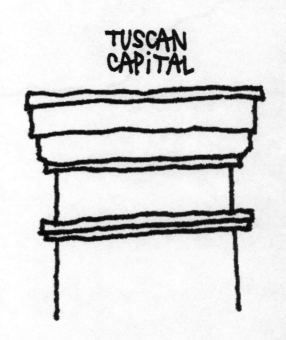

DORIC
CAPITAL

IONIC
CAPITAL

ROMANESQUE
CAPITAL

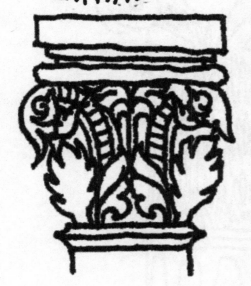

GOTHIC
CAPITAL

IONIC MODERN CAPITAL

CORINTHIAN CAPITAL

DRAW A CONTEMPORARY COLUMN WITH A CONTEMPORARY CAPITAL

RUINS

THESE RUINS ARE LISTED. RESTORE THEM TO THEIR FORMER GLORY

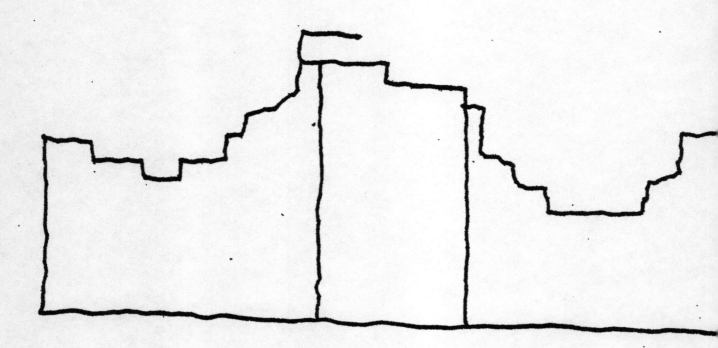

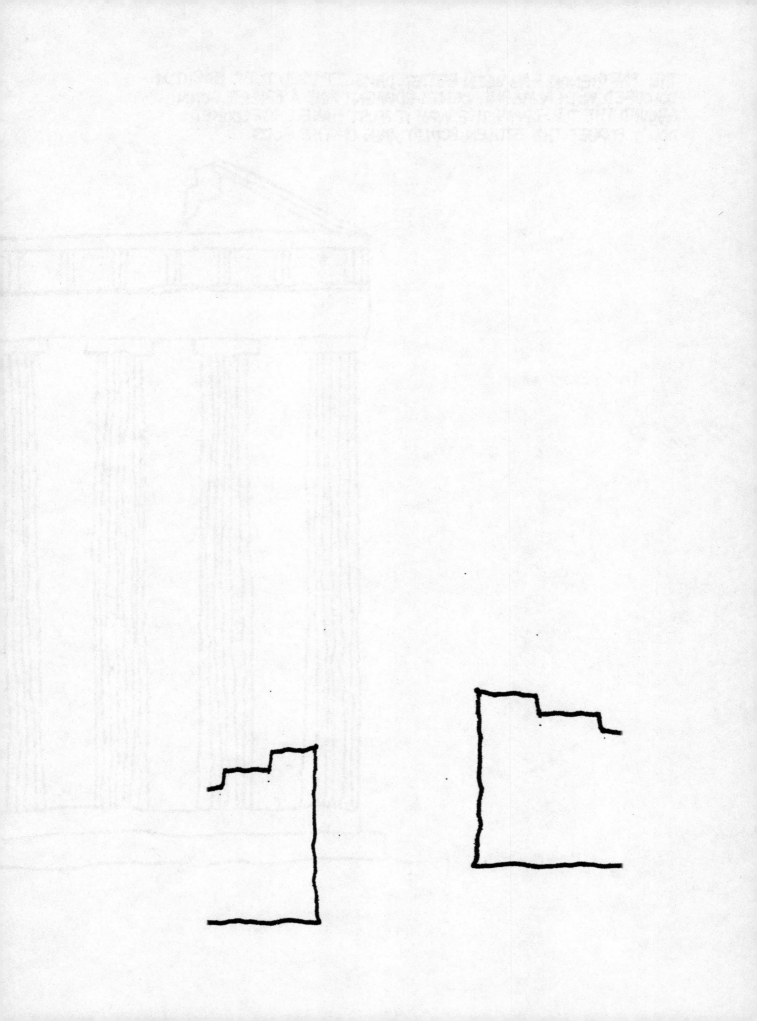

THE PARTHENON HAS SEEN BETTER DAYS. IT USED TO BE BRIGHTLY
COLOURED WITH A MAGNIFICENT PEDIMENT AND A FRIEZE RUNNING
AROUND THE TOP. DRAW THE WAY IT MUST HAVE ONCE LOOKED.
DON'T FORGET THE STOLEN SCULPTURES OF THE GODS

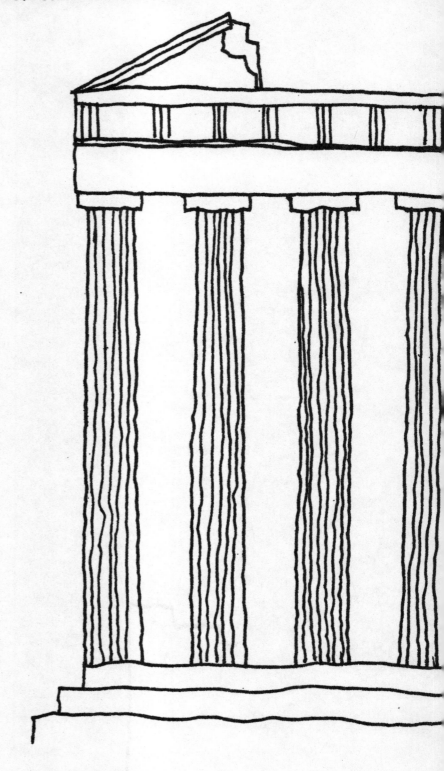

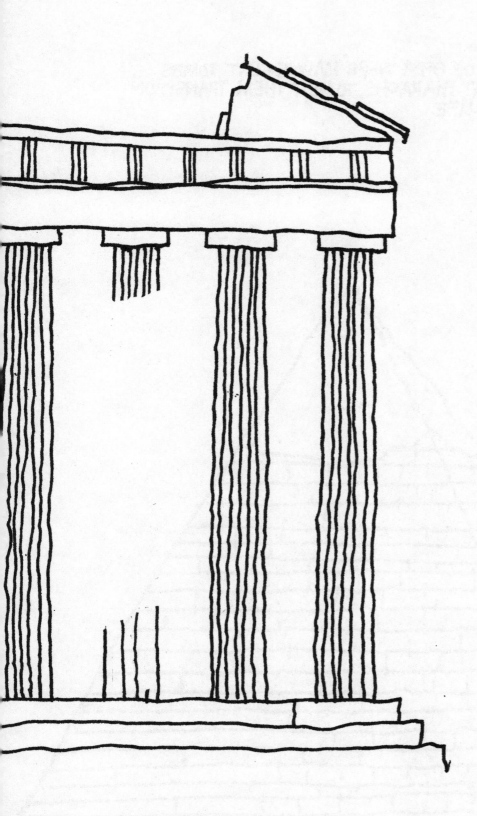

THE PYRAMIDS OF GIZA WERE MAGNIFICENT TOMBS,
FOR THE GREAT PHARAOHS, TO HELP THEM TRANSITION
TO THE AFTERLIFE

DRAW THE NOSE BACK ON THE SPHINX

DRAW A TOMB FOR A MODERN DAY PHARAOH

AQUEDUCT

THE ROMANS BUILT GREAT AQUEDUCTS TO SERVE ALL THE CORNERS
OF THEIR EMPIRE WITH DRINKING WATER AND PUBLIC BATHS.
THE ARCHES CREATE A LEVEL PITCH TO THE AQUEDUCT, SO THAT THE WATER
CAN FLOW OVER MANY MILES USING NOTHING BUT GRAVITY TO PROPEL IT

FINISH BUILDING THIS AQUEDUCT

BRIDGES

A SUSPENSION BRIDGE IS SUPPORTED BY CABLES
SUSPENDED BETWEEN TOWERS

THE CLIFTON SUSPENSION BRIDGE WAS THE LONGEST
SUSPENSION BRIDGE IN THE WORLD. IT WAS BUILT BY
ISAMABARD KINGDOM BRUNEL, AND WAS COMPLETED
IN 1864 - 32 YEARS AFTER WORK STARTED ON IT

THE RIALTO BRIDGE IN VENICE IS A SINGLE SPAN STONE BRIDGE.
THIS WAS ALSO A MIRACLE OF ENGINEERING WHEN IT WAS BUILT IN 1591

DRAW SOME OF THE GONDOLAS ON THE GRAND CANAL
THAT FLOWS UNDERNEATH THE BRIDGE

DRAW A LITTLE STONE BRIDGE OVER THIS PRETTY STREAM

DRAW A GREAT BIG BRIDGE OVER THIS PRECIPITOUS GORGE

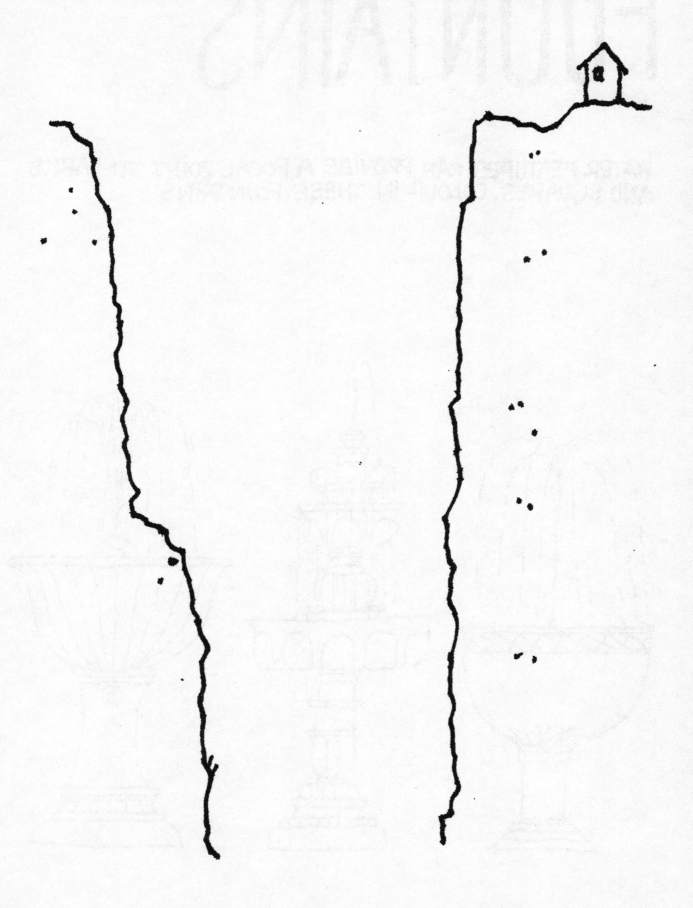

FOUNTAINS

WATER FEATURES CAN PROVIDE A FOCAL POINT TO PARKS AND SQUARES. COLOUR IN THESE FOUNTAINS

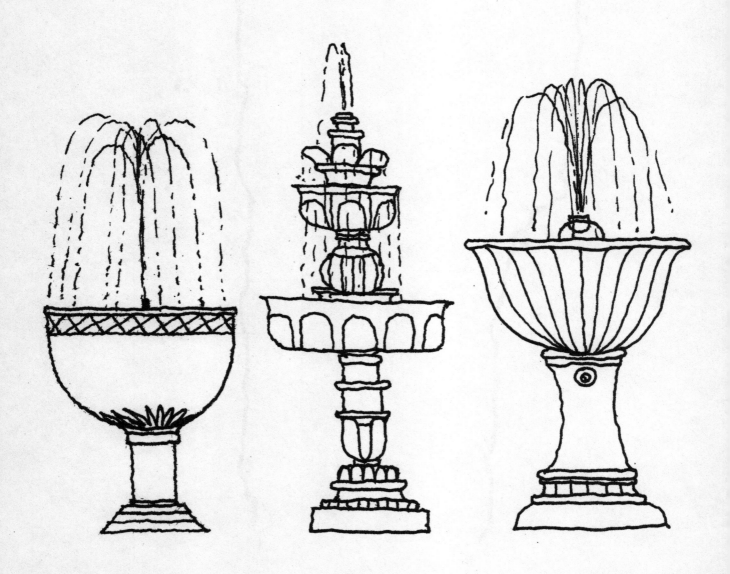

DRAW THE WATER JETS ON THIS FOUNTAIN

THIS IS LONDON'S TRAFALGAR SQUARE FROM ABOVE.
NELSON'S COLUMN TOWERS OVER THE SPACE, AND
THERE ARE THREE FURTHER STATUES ON PLINTHS

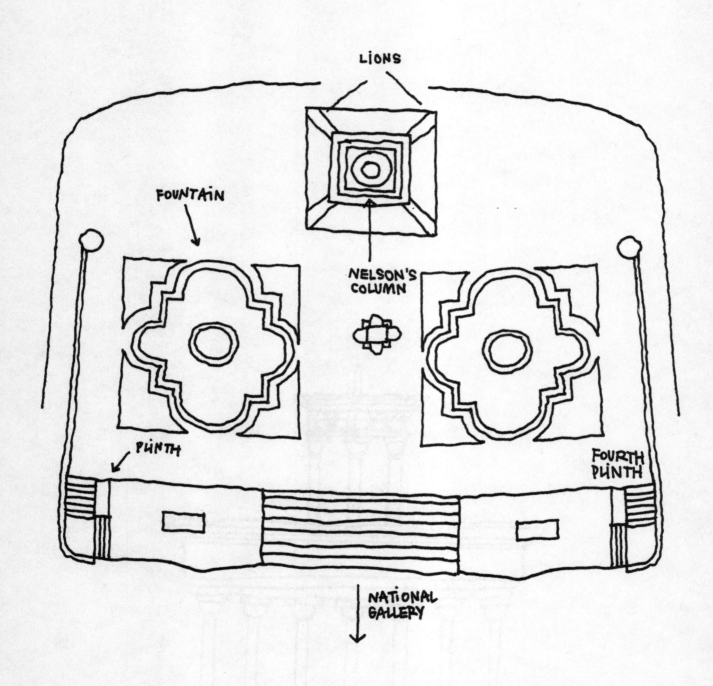

LIONS

FOUNTAIN

NELSON'S
COLUMN

PLINTH

FOURTH
PLINTH

NATIONAL
GALLERY

THE FOURTH PLINTH IS LEFT EMPTY FOR COMMISSIONED
ARTWORKS BY CONTEMPORARY ARTISTS.
WHAT WOULD YOU PUT THERE?

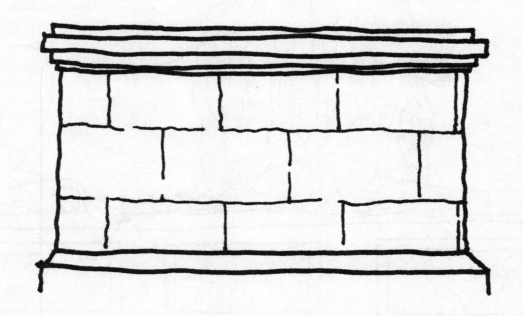

THERE ARE FOUR LIONS AT THE BASE
OF NELSON'S COLUMN IN TRAFALGAR SQUARE

WHAT WOULD THE COLUMN LOOK LIKE
WITH A DIFFERENT ANIMAL AT ITS BASE ?

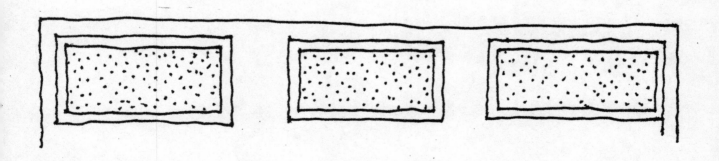

OUR PERSPECTIVES CHANGE DEPENDING
ON WHERE WE'RE STANDING

THIS IS THE MOON FROM EARTH

THIS IS THE EARTH FROM THE MOON

CHANGE YOUR PERSPECTIVE ON WHERE YOU ARE.
DRAW AN AERIAL VIEW OF THE ROOM YOU'RE STANDING IN

MEMORIALS ARE MONUMENTS BUILT TO
COMMEMORATE A PERSON OR AN EVENT
THAT HAD AN IMPACT ON OUR SOCIETY

THE HOLOCAUST MEMORIAL IN BERLIN,
DESIGNED BY PETER EISENMAN,
COMPLETED IN 2004

THE LINCOLN MEMORIAL IN WASHINGTON,
DESIGNED BY HENRY BACON, COMPLETED IN 1922

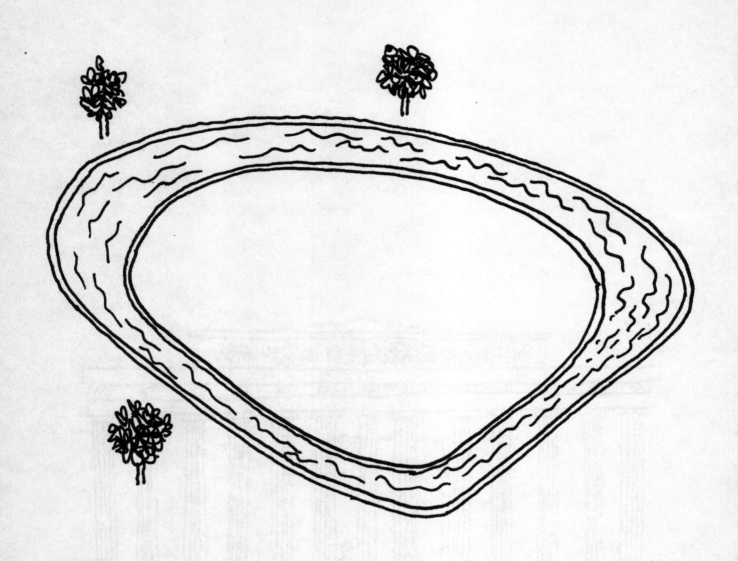

DIANA MEMORIAL FOUNTAIN
DESIGNED BY KATHRYN GUSTAFSON
COMPLETED IN 2004

DRAW A MEMORIAL TO A RECENT EVENT

ROOFS

TO HAVE A SHELTER, THE FIRST THING YOU NEED IS A ROOF, TO PROTECT YOU FROM EXTREMES OF RAIN, SNOW AND SUN. ROOFS HAVE DIFFERENT REQUIREMENTS FOR DIFFERENT TYPES OF SHELTER

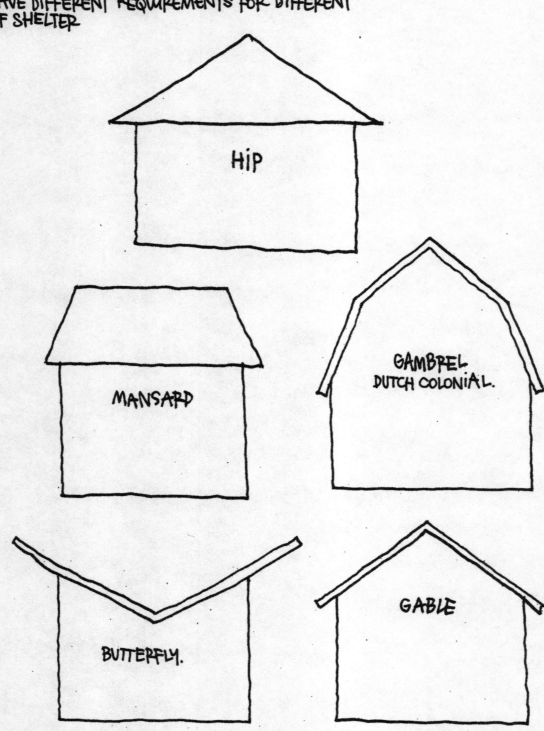

HIP

MANSARD

GAMBREL
DUTCH COLONIAL.

BUTTERFLY.

GABLE

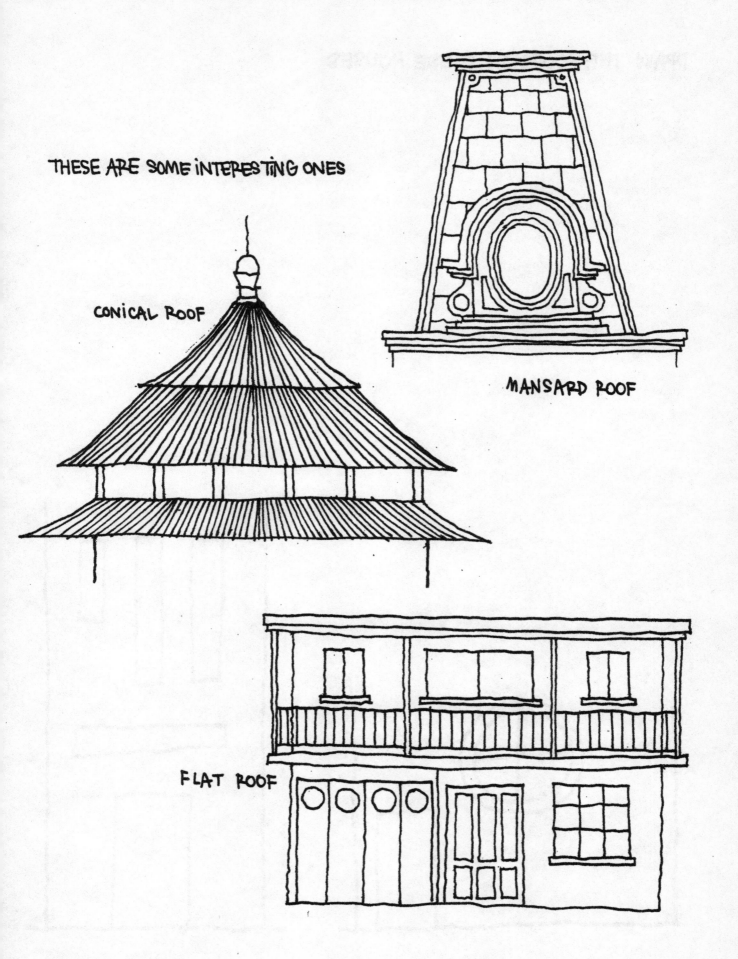

THESE ARE SOME INTERESTING ONES

CONICAL ROOF

MANSARD ROOF

FLAT ROOF

DRAW THE ROOFS ON THESE HOUSES

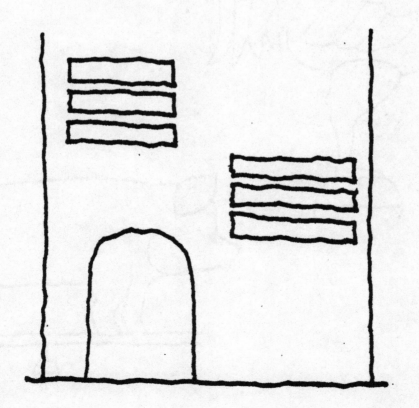

WEATHER VANES SHOW WHICH DIRECTION
THE WIND IS BLOWING. THEY CAN BE IN THE SHAPE OF ANIMALS...

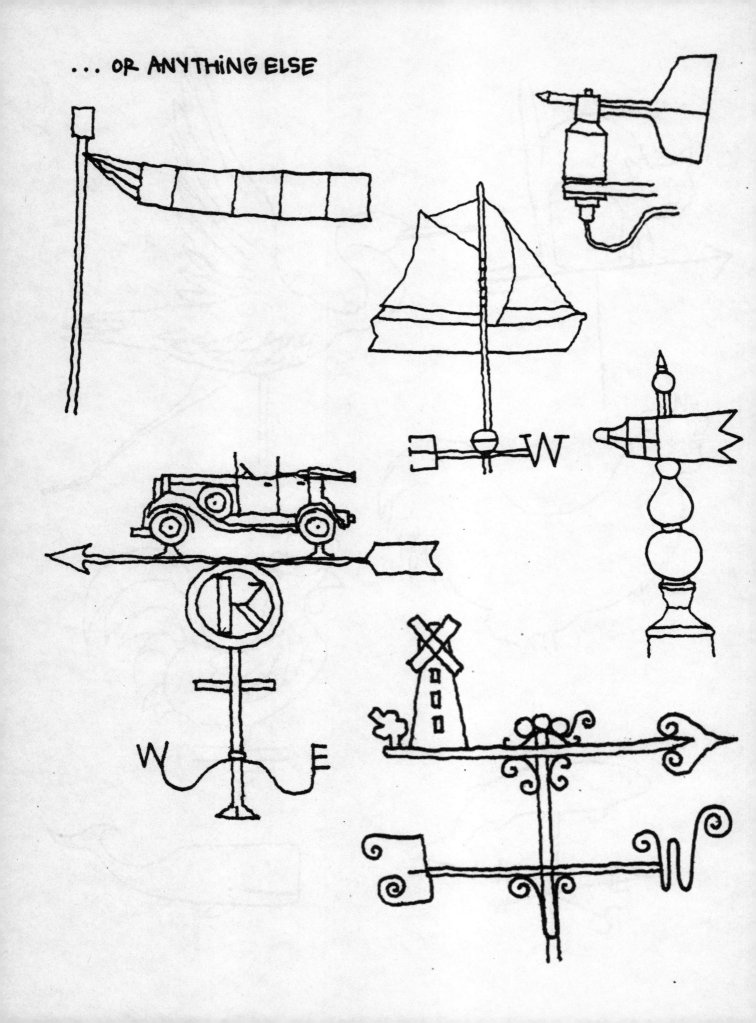

WHICH WAY IS YOUR WIND BLOWING?
DRAW YOUR OWN WEATHER VANE HERE

EXTEN-SIONS

SOMETIMES OLD BUILDINGS NEED TO BE CHANGED OR EXTENDED
TO MEET NEW REQUIREMENTS.

THESE PYRAMIDS OUTSIDE THE LOUVRE
IN PARIS WERE DESIGNED BY I·M·PEI SO THAT THE NEW
UNDERGROUND LOBBY COULD ACCOMMODATE THE CROWDS OF VISITORS

THIS VICTORIAN TERRACE WAS EXTENDED AT THE BACK
TO CREATE A BIGGER FAMILY SPACE

THE BILBAO GUGGENHEIM, DESIGNED BY FRANK GEHRY IS A PRETTY RADICAL BUILDING.

CAN YOU DESIGN A RADICAL EXTENSION TO MATCH?

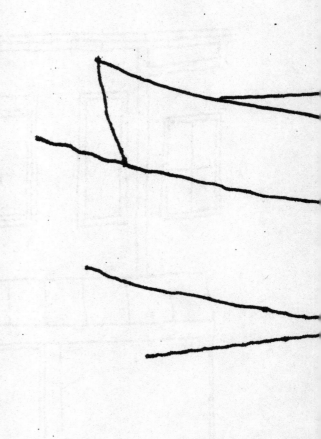

EXTEND THIS FAMILY HOME TO THE SIDE
TO MAKE SPACE FOR GRANNY TO MOVE IN

AN ARCHITECT HAS TO LOOK AT THE FOOTPRINT OF A BUILDING AND THINK CREATIVELY ABOUT HOW THE SPACE CAN BE USED

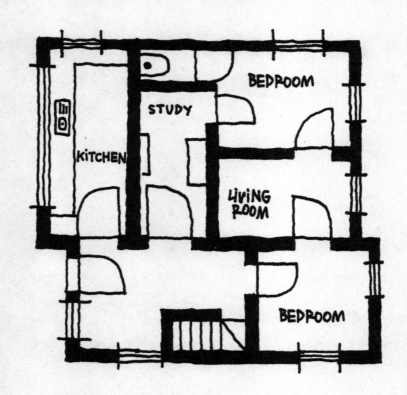

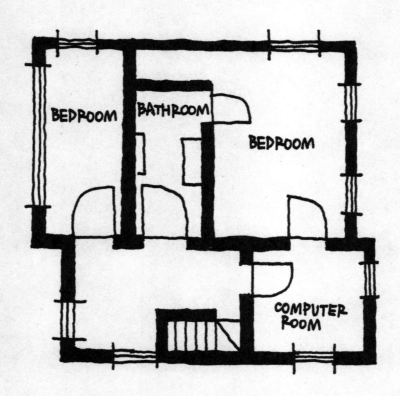

THIS IS THE FOOTPRINT OF A FOUR-BEDROOMED HOUSE.
HOW WOULD YOU REARRANGE THE SPACE SO THAT THERE
ARE FEWER BEDROOMS BUT MORE LIVING SPACE?

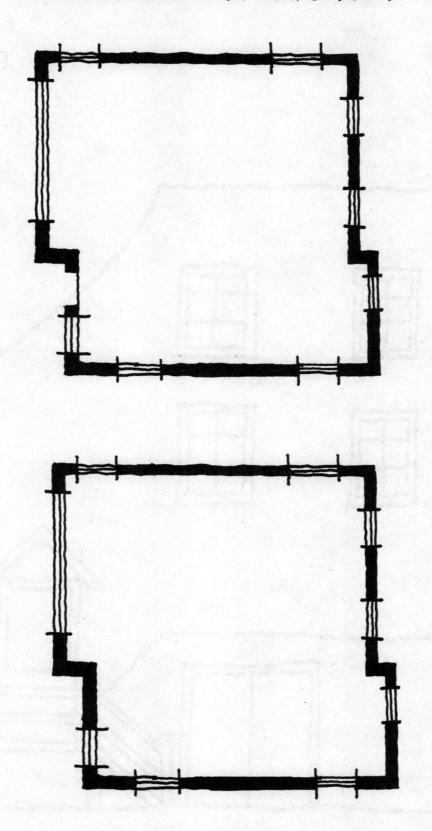

CAN YOU DRAW A HOUSE IN THE SHAPE OF A HAT?
22. HOW ABOUT A PROCESS?

SOMETIMES CLIENTS ASK ARCHITECTS TO DESIGN REALLY
WACKY HOUSES. THIS ONE IN THE SHAPE OF A SHOE

CAN YOU DRAW A HOUSE IN THE SHAPE OF A HAT?
OR HOW ABOUT A SPACESHIP?

DRAW THE PEOPLE WHO MiGHT WANT
TO LiVE iN THOSE HOUSES

VICTORIAN INTERIORS WERE VERY DECORATIVE. THESE ARE SOME ELEMENTS THE VICTORIANS MIGHT HAVE HAD IT THEIR HOMES

FIREPLACE

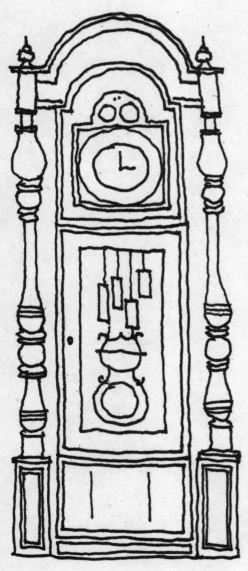

GRANDFATHER CLOCK.

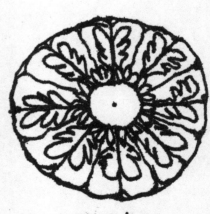

CEILING ROSE

DRESSING TABLE

CHAISE LONGUE

RESTORE THE ORIGINAL FEATURES TO THIS ROOM
AND FURNISH IT WITH VICTORIAN OBJECTS.
<u>HELP</u>: IN VICTORIAN TIMES, PEOPLE LIKED THEIR
HOUSE TO BE COLOURFUL

Published by Cicada Books Limited

Illustrated and designed by Thibaud Herem
Edited by Ziggy Hanaor

British Library Cataloguing-in-Publication Data.

A CIP record for this book is available from the British Library.
ISBN: 978-0-9562053-7-7

© 2012 Cicada Books Limited

Cicada Books Limited
85 Parkhill Road
London
NW3 2XY

T: +44 207 267 5208
E: ziggy@cicadabooks.co.uk
W: www.cicadabooks.co.uk1]

Printed in China